Survey Responses From Region 5:
Are We Achieving the Public's Objectives for
Forests and Rangelands?

Donna L. Lybecker and Deborah J. Shields

U.S. Department of Agriculture   Forest Service

Lybecker, Donna L., Shields, Deborah J. 2005. **Survey responses from Region 5: Are we achieving the public's objectives for forests and rangelands?** Gen. Tech. Rep. RMRS-GTR-157. Fort Collins, CO: U.S. Department of Agriculture, Forest Service, Rocky Mountain Research Station. 32 p.

Abstract

The survey on values, objectives, beliefs, and attitudes, implemented as a module of the National Survey on Recreation and the Environment, asked over 7,000 respondents nationwide about their values with respect to public lands, objectives for the management of these lands, beliefs about the role the USDA Forest Service should play in fulfilling those objectives, and attitudes about the job the agency has been doing. This report—one of a series of similar regional reports—shows respondents from the Pacific Southwest (USDA Forest Service Region 5: California and Hawaii) are quite similar to those of the rest of the United States, although respondents from the Pacific Southwest show a stronger tendency towards allowing access for diverse uses and are slightly less inclined toward informing the public. Nationwide, as in the Pacific Southwest, the most important objective was conserving and protecting forests and grassland watersheds.

Other reports in the series *Are We Achieving the Public's Objectives for Forests and Rangelands?*

- *Survey Responses From Region 3* (Arizona and New Mexico) RMRS-GTR-156

- *Survey Responses From Region 8* (Alabama, Arkansas, Florida, Georgia, Kentucky, Louisiana, Mississippi, North Carolina, Oklahoma, Puerto Rico, South Carolina, Tennessee, Texas, Virginia) RMRS-GTR-158

- *Survey Responses From Region 9* (Connecticut, Delaware, Illinois, Indiana, Iowa, Maine, Maryland, Massachusetts, Michigan, Minnesota, Missouri, New Hampshire, New Jersey, New York, Ohio, Pennsylvania, Rhode Island, Vermont, West Virginia, Wisconsin) RMRS-GTR-159

- *Survey Responses From the Intermountain West* (Arizona, Colorado, Idaho, Montana, Nevada, New Mexico, Utah, Wyoming) RMRS-GTR-160

- Comparison of 2000/2003 Data – Forthcoming

Survey Responses From Region 5:
Are We Achieving the Public's Objectives for Forests and Rangelands?

Donna L. Lybecker and Deborah J. Shields

Contents

Introduction

The mission of the USDA Forest Service is twofold: caring for the land and serving people. Because personal satisfaction is an individual concept with multiple facets, providing high-quality customer service and achieving high levels of customer satisfaction can be as challenging as managing for healthy ecosystems.

A person's attitudes about the Forest Service are often influenced by the nature and outcomes of his or her interactions with Forest Service employees. Were they polite, knowledgeable, helpful, professional? Was the process straightforward, efficient, prompt, and fair? Was the desired outcome achieved, such as acquiring a fuelwood permit or getting information on day hikes? Although traditional customer satisfaction surveys do a good job of collecting this type of information, they tend to focus on delivery of services to specific classes of "users" (for example, permittees or applicants for timber sales or grazing allotments), and are not designed to capture the preferences and attitudes of the broader public.

In addition to personal interactions with the Forest Service, people's perceptions of the agency are also influenced by their attitudes about how and toward what end the Forest Service manages public land. Various segments of the public have both general and in some cases quite detailed objectives related to the health of forests and rangelands, how Forest Service lands should be managed, and the activities that should be allowed to take place on them. If stakeholders observe that an objective they deem important is not being fulfilled, their satisfaction with the Forest Service may be lowered regardless of the quality of their interactions with individual Forest Service employees or their experience with the agency's other protocols. Thus, understanding the public's objectives and comparing them with the agency's objectives can provide useful input to the strategic planning process.

This report describes the public's values, objectives, beliefs, and attitudes for and toward the USDA Forest Service, with particular focus on Region 5, the Pacific Southwest (California and Hawaii). Information on the public's perceptions has been collected through an ongoing survey entitled "The American Public's Values, Objectives, Beliefs, and Attitudes Regarding Forests and Rangelands" (hereafter VOBA). The VOBA survey asked respondents about their environmental values as they relate to public lands, their objectives for the management of forests and rangelands in general as well as those managed by the Forest Service, their beliefs about whether it is the role of the Forest Service to fulfill these objectives, and their attitudes about the performance of the agency in fulfilling these objectives. This report compares the nation-wide public's responses to those from respondents in Region 5. Results show strong parallels between the views of respondents from Region 5 and those of respondents from the rest of the United States. One difference, however, is that compared to public from the rest of the United States, the public from Region 5 is less likely to believe that fulfilling the goals of the stated objectives are appropriate roles for the USDA Forest Service.

This report is organized as follows. First there is a brief discussion of the data used in the analysis. The following section outlines the methods used to analyze the American public's values, objectives, beliefs, and attitudes regarding forests and rangelands. Next, results for Region 5 are reported. Finally, responses from Region 5 are compared with those from the rest of the United States.

Data and Methodology

Data for this report come from the VOBA survey. The survey was implemented as a module of the National Survey on Recreation and the Environment (NSRE). This random telephone survey was administered for the USDA Forest Service by the University of Tennessee. Although random, it is important to note that a telephone survey such as the NSRE will not adequately represent the views of segments of the population that do not have access to or choose not to have telephones. In addition to the VOBA questions, respondents were asked about their recreational behaviors and basic demographics.

The VOBA part of the survey is comprised of statements to which respondents indicate their level of agreement or approval in four areas—values, objectives, beliefs, and attitudes—regarding forests and rangelands. Respondents indicate their agreement or approval on a five-point scale. The objectives scale items are anchored by 1=not at all important and 5=very important. The Value and Belief scale items are anchored by 1=strongly disagree and 5=strongly agree. The Attitude scale items are anchored by 1=very unfavorable and 5=very favorable.

The VOBA surveys objectives, and related beliefs and attitudes; it does not directly ask respondents about their opinions of the USDA Forest Service goals, as embodied in the Forest Service 2000 Strategic Plan. Likewise, the survey does not ask for an individual's reaction to the Chief's Agenda or Leadership Team priorities. The VOBA objectives statements were developed during a series of 80 focus group meetings conducted with members of various stakeholder groups as well as individuals throughout the country. As such, they represent the main objectives for land management as they were presented to us by the public.

An objectives hierarchy constructed for each of the focus groups indicated the group's goals for the management of forests and rangelands, and how they would like to see each goal or objective achieved. The objectives ranged from the abstract strategic level to the more focused or applied means level (figure 1).

The strategic level objectives are abstract, while fundamental level objectives represent a context-specific application of strategic objectives. End-state fundamental objectives represent the desired state of the world. Fundamental means objectives capture the methods by which the desired end-state should be achieved.

The objectives elicited from all the focus groups were pooled, duplications eliminated, and overlaps accounted for. Five strategic-level objectives were consistently revealed: Access, Preservation/ Conservation, Economic Development, Education, and Natural Resource Management. The 30 items in the VOBA objectives scale are the fundamental objectives that indicate both end-state preferences and the means by which they should be

achieved. Each correlates to one of the strategic objectives. Objectives may be applicable only at the regional or national scale, be location specific, or be meaningful at multiple scales. The VOBA survey objectives are applicable to the management of forests and rangelands at a broad geographic scale. Many of the objectives are also meaningful at the regional level. However, the public may have additional objectives specific to home region that are not captured in the existing national survey instrument.

The belief and attitude statements tier down directly from the objectives. For example an objective might be "more hiking trails." The corresponding belief question asks whether the respondent believes that providing more hiking trails is an appropriate role for the USDA Forest Service. The attitude question would then elicit input on the respondent's perception of how well the agency is doing at providing hiking trails.

The value scale in the VOBA survey differs from other value survey instruments in that it focuses on values associated with public lands. It is applicable at multiple spatial scales, and in addition to being used in the national VOBA survey, has been applied at the National Forest scale.

The Public Lands Values scale was developed using approximately 200 items that, through a series of iterations using both student and adult samples around the United States, were reduced to a 25-item scale. This scale was designed to focus on values that people hold for the environment in general and public lands in particular. It has been tested on four National Forests in Colorado (Arapaho, Roosevelt, Pike, and San Isabel) using various traditional and non-traditional stakeholder groups. Past research and testing have shown that responses to the Public Lands Values scale can be arranged into two categories: Socially Responsible Individual Values (SRIV) and Socially Responsible Management Values (SRMV).

Finally, it is important to note that the wording of the statements within the VOBA was designed with public lands in mind. Thus some statements may raise questions concerning the appropriateness of the language for private lands. In other words, the language used may not be applicable to some types of private land use concerns, making it less appropriate to draw overarching conclusions about general land management. For example, the objective, "Developing and maintaining continuous trail systems that cross both public and private land for motorized vehicles such as snowmobiles or ATVs," is written with public land managers in mind. A similar objective,

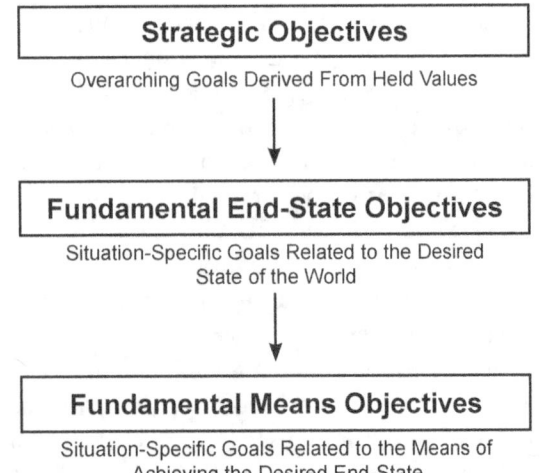

Figure 1—Objectives Hierarchy.

written from the perspective of private landowners, might say something like, "Coordinating with public and private actors to support and maintain continuous trail systems that cross both public and private land for motorized vehicles." Although the wording for many of the objectives does not present this concern, it is necessary to remain aware that respondents may be thinking solely of public lands instead of both public and private lands when responding to some of the objectives.[1]

Data Collection

The VOBA survey was implemented as a module of the NSRE, a survey with a nationwide sample. Of the 7,069 nationwide respondents, 636 came from Region 5. The number of responses in any region is a function of the overall VOBA sampling design. The data were collected between late 1999 and early 2000. For each State the size of the sample was proportional to its population. Due to a limited amount of time available for each phone interview, participants were asked to respond to only a portion of the full set of VOBA questions. Each respondent was asked about one fundamental objective from each of the five strategic level objective categories. Due to this sampling design, each item in the objectives, beliefs, and attitude scales has fewer than the full 636 respondents.

The overall goal of this split sampling design was to control interview time with respondents, yet collect analytically valuable information. This not only lowers costs, but also reduces respondent burden, which should lead to fewer non-responses and therefore to a better sample quality.[2] To ensure high confidence levels, the full national survey was designed so that there was a minimum of 700 responses for each question. This design generates response numbers for each question that are adequate to support multivariate statistical analysis, and provides a high level of confidence in the results. In Region 5 the response numbers for each question ranged from 55 to 210. As a result of this smaller sample size, there is a slightly greater chance the results do not fully reflect the precise traits of the region; however, the sample size is still large enough to give a relatively high level of confidence in the results.

Methodology

The objective of this analysis is to determine the important and unimportant objectives, the perceived appropriateness of roles for the USDA Forest Service, the favorable or unfavorable view of the agency's performance, and the uniformly held socially responsible individual and management values. Descriptive statistics, mean, standard deviation, and frequency distribution, were calculated for each of the 115 objective, belief, and attitude statements. Factor scores (group means) were calculated for the values statements and, where appropriate, items were reverse scored (see Appendix).

Results for Region 5: Objectives, Beliefs, and Attitudes_____

Results from Region 5 respondents to the VOBA national survey are reported first for *objectives*, the extent to which the public believes it is the job of the Forest Service to fulfill the objectives (*beliefs*), and the perception of agency performance in fulfilling these objectives (*attitudes*). These results are grouped as to objectives the Region 5 public feels are the most important, not important, and moderately important. For each of these groups of objectives the level of consensus (or lack thereof) among the public is also highlighted.

Results for the *value*s are then divided into Socially Responsible Individual Public Lands Values with a high level of agreement among Region 5 respondents, Socially Responsible Individual Public Lands Values with a low level of agreement among respondents, and Socially Responsible Management Values.

Objectives Identified as Important

For this report, a mean response of 4.00 or greater (out of a possible 5) indicates an objective is important to the respondents in Region 5. Additionally, the objectives determined to be important are divided into core important objectives and other important objectives, determined by the standard deviation (s.d.) of less than 1.00 or greater than or equal to 1.00, respectively.

---

[1] For more detailed information on the survey, see Shields, D., M. Martin, W. Martin, and M. Haefele. 2002. *Survey Results of the American Public's Values, Objectives, Beliefs, and Attitudes Regarding Forests and Grasslands.* Gen. Tech. Rep. RMRS-GTR-95. Fort Collins, CO: U.S. Department of Agriculture, Forest Service, Rocky Mountain Research Station.

[2] For more information on split sampling designs, see for example, Raghunathan, T.E. and Grizzle, J.E. 1995. "A Split Questionnaire Survey Design," *Journal of the American Statistical Association*, 90: 54-63.

Twelve of the original 30 objectives were thus identified as important to the people of Region 5. Six of these 12 were further specified as "core" objectives, because their response ratings had a standard deviation (s.d.) of less than 1.00, indicating that the public is generally in agreement about the importance of these objectives.[3]

Core Important Objectives

The six core objectives for the public in Region 5 are presented in detail in table 1. For each of the six core objectives, a histogram compares the distribution of responses for the importance of the objective, the agency role, and customer satisfaction. In each case there is agreement that the objective is important, and that it is an appropriate role for the USDA Forest Service. However, this consistency does not hold when looking at agency performance. None of these objectives show a public with a "very favorable" or "favorable" (mean above 4.00) view of the performance of the USDA Forest Service.

Watershed protection—The VOBA objective deemed the most important by respondents in Region 5 is the conservation and protection of lands that are the source of our water resources. This objective has a mean of 4.68 and a standard deviation of 0.85 (table 1; figure 2), which shows the distribution of responses. The mean of 4.66

Table 1--Core important objectives for respondents from Region 5.

OBJECTIVE:	Is this an important objective for you? *(1=not at all important, 5=very important)*	Do you believe that fulfilling this objective is an appropriate role for the USDA Forest Service? *(1=strongly disagree, 5=strongly agree)*	How favorably do you view the performance of the USDA Forest Service in fulfilling this objective? *(1=very unfavorably, 5=very favorably)*
Conserving and protecting forests and grasslands that are the source of our water resources, such as streams, lakes, and watershed areas.	4.68 *0.85*[a] *95*[b]	4.66 *0.77* *120*	3.75 *1.09* *113*
Informing the public about recreation concerns on forests and grasslands such as safety, trail etiquette, and respect for wildlife.	4.65 *0.74* *89*	4.44 *0.98* *106*	3.79 *1.24* *111*
Protecting ecosystems and wildlife habitats.	4.61 *0.77* *132*	4.74 *0.67* *112*	3.79 *1.02* *110*
Developing volunteer programs to improve forests and grasslands (for example, planting trees, or improving water quality).	4.56 *0.93* *118*	4.51 *0.91* *102*	3.56 *1.23* *77*
Developing volunteer programs to maintain trails and facilities on forests and grasslands (for example, trail maintenance or campground maintenance).	4.24 *0.97* *85*	4.40 *0.87* *91*	3.68 *1.28* *80*
Allowing for diverse uses of forests and grasslands such as grazing, recreation, and wildlife habitat.	4.03 *0.98* *94*	4.07 *1.21* *75*	3.66 *1.08* *58*

[a] Standard deviation
[b] Sample size for each item (n) The sample sizes for each item are less than the full 636 sample since each respondent was asked only a portion of the 115 VOBA questions due to time limitations

---

[3] General agreement about the importance of these objectives is revealed with the standard deviation. The standard deviation is defined as the average amount by which scores in a distribution differ from the mean; it offers an indication of the spread of the data. For example, when looking at the importance of a given objective, the standard deviation reveals how tightly all the responses are clustered around the mean score for the stated objective. This helps to reveal if there are extreme responses or if most respondents agreed on their rating.

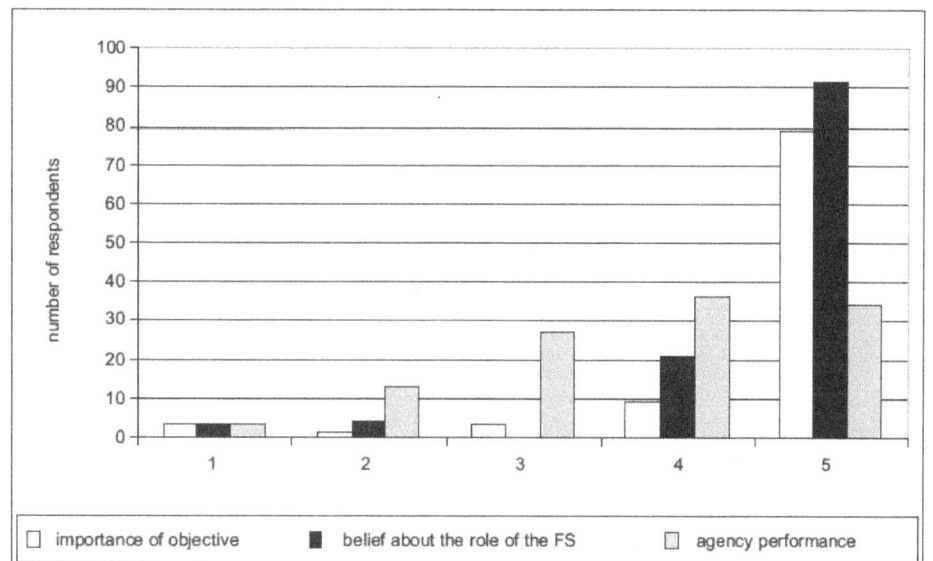

Figure 2—Distribution of Objectives, Beliefs, and Attitude scores for: Conserving and protecting forests and grasslands that are the source of our water resources, such as streams, lakes, and watershed areas.

for the corresponding belief statement also indicates that the public considers the protection of watersheds to be an appropriate role for the USDA Forest Service. This belief has wide consensus as well, indicated by the standard deviation of 0.77. Agency performance is viewed by Region 5 respondents as somewhat favorable, with a mean of 3.75. This rating, however, does not exhibit as much consensus as the objective and belief (s.d. 1.09).

Recreation concerns—The second-most important core objective for the public of Region 5 is the distribution of information about recreation concerns, with a mean of 4.65. The standard deviation of 0.74 indicates general consensus about the importance of this core

objective (figure 3). The distribution of this type of information is also viewed as an appropriate role for the agency (mean 4.44, s.d. 0.98). Agency performance is viewed as somewhat favorable (mean 3.79), but there is wide disagreement about this evaluation (s.d. 1.24).

Protecting ecosystems— The mean of 4.61 and standard deviation of 0.77 for protection of ecosystems and wildlife habitats reveal not only the importance of this objective, but also a high level of consensus among the respondents from Region 5 for this evaluation (figure 4). There is also wide agreement among these respondents that the protection of ecosystems and wildlife habitats are an appropriate role for the USDA Forest

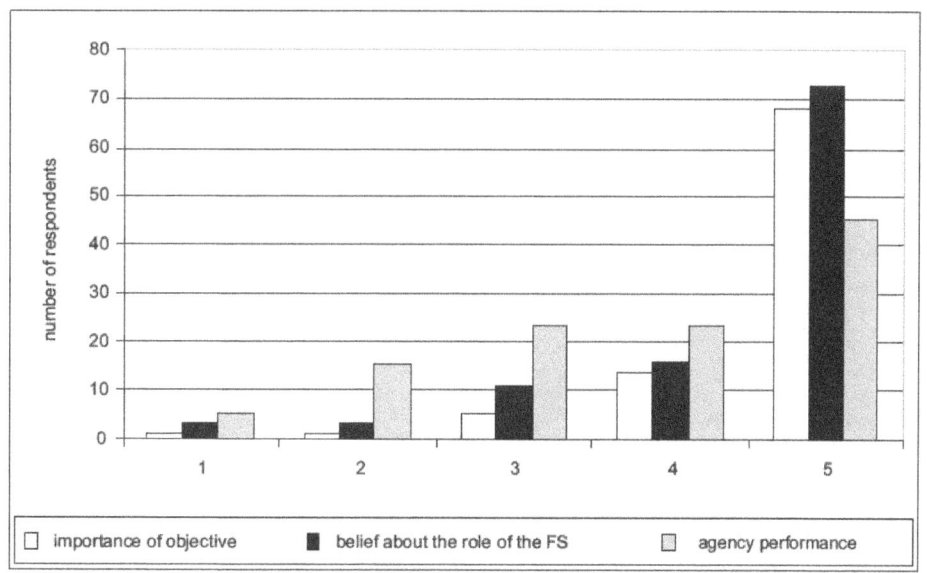

Figure 3—Distribution of Objectives, Beliefs, and Attitude scores for: Informing the public about recreation concerns on forests and grasslands such as safety, trail etiquette, and respect for wildlife.

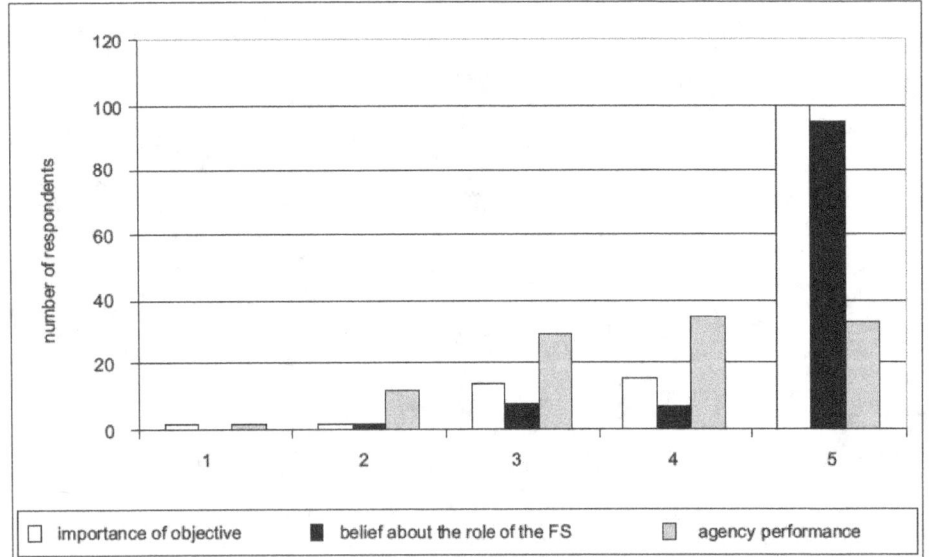

Figure 4—Distribution of Objectives, Beliefs, and Attitude scores for: Protecting ecosystems and wildlife habitats.

Service (mean 4.74, s.d. 0.67). However, the assessment of agency performance had a mean of only 3.79 (s.d. 1.02).

Volunteer programs—The development of two types of volunteer programs is also highly important to the respondents from Region 5. The first of these, developing volunteer programs to improve the heath of forests and grasslands, has a mean of 4.56 and a standard deviation of 0.93. This indicates wide agreement that these programs are important. The Region 5 respondents also see the development of these volunteer programs as an appropriate role for the agency (mean 4.51) and the standard deviation of 0.91 reveals greater

agreement concerning appropriateness of the agency role than with the objective itself. Finally, this objective has the lowest performance evaluation of the six core objectives—although the evaluation is still somewhat favorable (mean 3.56). This evaluation has a high standard deviation (1.23) indicating that the respondents' attitudes vary widely. Figure 5 shows that the majority of respondents from Region 5 view agency performance as adequate, although nearly 69% (the percentage of respondents answering 4 or less) feel that the agency could be doing a better job.

The development of volunteer programs to maintain trails and facilities within forests and grasslands is also

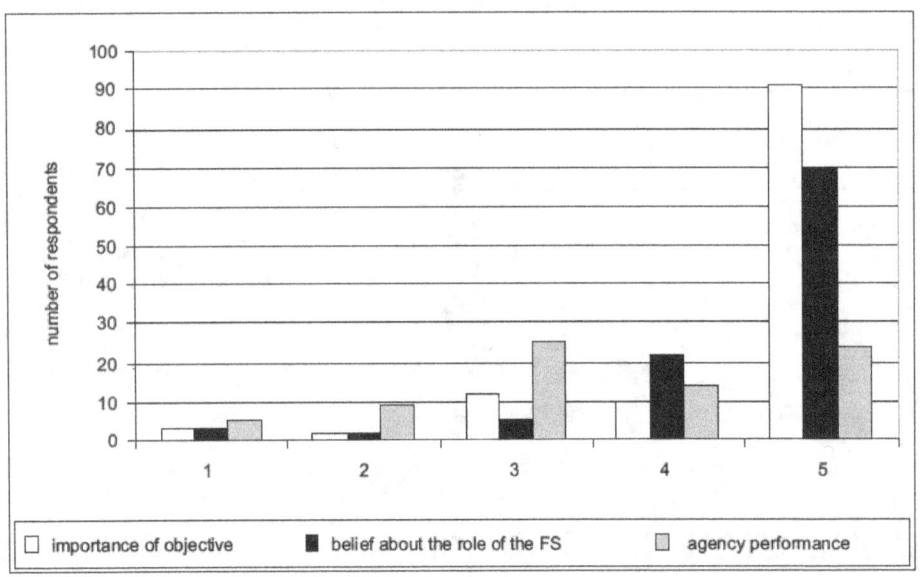

Figure 5—Distribution of Objectives, Beliefs, and Attitude scores for: Developing volunteer programs to improve forests and grasslands (for example, planting trees, or improving water quality).

USDA Forest Service RMRS-GTR-157. 2005.

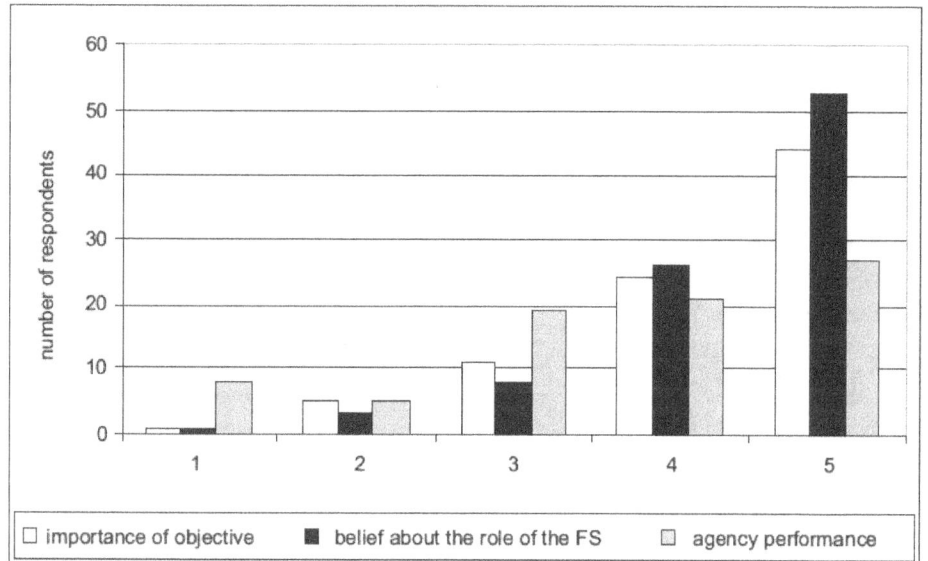

Figure 6—Distribution of Objectives, Beliefs, and Attitude scores for: Developing volunteer programs to maintain trails and facilities on forests and grasslands (for example, trail maintenance or campground maintenance).

evaluated to be highly important for the respondents of Region 5 (figure 6). The mean of 4.24 and the standard deviation of 0.97 reveal agreement on the importance of developing such volunteer program. Development of these programs is also seen as an appropriate role for the USDA Forest Service (mean 4.40, s.d. 0.87). Finally, as with the development of other volunteer programs, agency performance is somewhat favorable (mean 3.68), although the high standard deviation (1.28) indicates the respondents' attitudes vary greatly.

Diverse uses—Most respondents in Region 5 rate allowing for diverse uses as a core objective (mean 4.03, s.d. 0.98). As with the other core objectives, respondents

see this as an appropriate role for the USDA Forest Service (mean 4.07), but there is some disagreement about this assessment (s.d. 1.21). This may indicate that some respondents would prefer to see the agency limit uses allowed within forests and grasslands. Agency performance is viewed by Region 5 respondents as somewhat favorable, with a mean of 3.66, but the standard deviation (1.08) indicates some dissenting voices. Figure 7 shows that while the majority of respondents view the objective as important and its fulfillment as an appropriate role for the agency, more than 74% (the percentage of respondents answering 4 or less) felt the agency could be doing a better job.

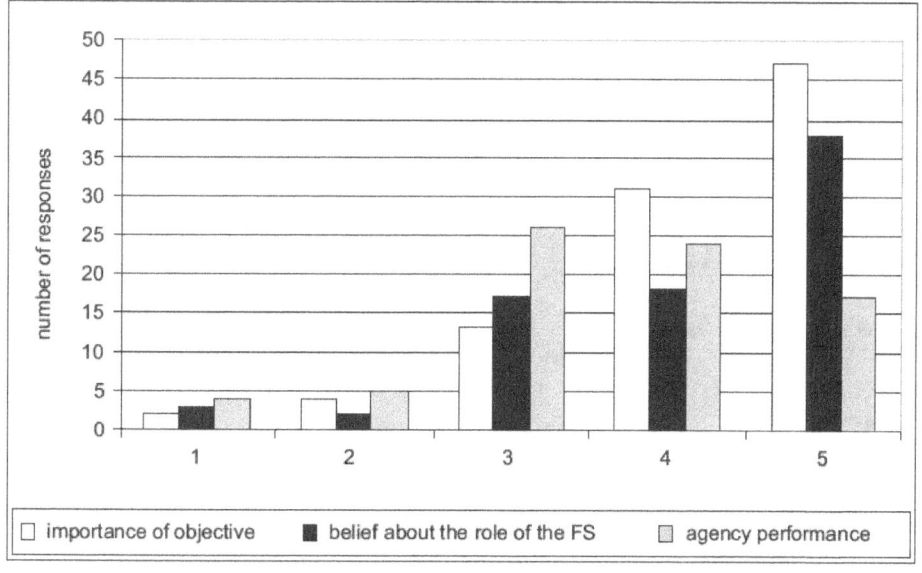

Figure 7—Distribution of Objectives, Beliefs, and Attitude scores for: Allowing for diverse uses of forests and grasslands such as grazing, recreation, and wildlife habitat.

Other Important Objectives

Table 2 shows the distribution of scores for the other objectives respondents in Region 5 felt were important. These six objectives are viewed as important, based on means over 4.00, but their standard deviations are greater than or equal to 1.00, indicating a greater diversity of responses. The objectives in table 2 are arranged by standard deviation: lowest standard deviation (higher consensus) to highest standard deviation (less consensus). As a result, some objectives identified as relatively more important are lower in the table than some objectives identified as relatively less important. Each of these objectives will be discussed briefly.

Preserving the wilderness experience—Preserving the ability to have a 'wilderness' experience has a mean of 4.26 and a standard deviation of 1.00, indicating some consensus for the evaluation, although less than for the core objectives. The public in Region 5 sees this as an appropriate role for the USDA Forest Service (mean 4.32), but there are some dissenting voices as indicated by the standard deviation (1.02). Agency performance is

seen as somewhat favorable (mean 3.86), but again there is some disagreement (s.d. 1.17). (See figure 8.)

Informing the public—Informing the public on potential environmental impacts is also important to the people of Region 5 (mean 4.24), although there is a lack of consistency in this evaluation (s.d. 1.10). Informing the public of potential environmental impacts is seen as an appropriate role for the agency (mean 4.51), and there is wide agreement about this assessment (s.d. 0.89). Agency performance is seen as somewhat favorable (mean 3.22), although the high standard deviation (1.37) again indicates substantial disagreement. The histogram (figure 9) shows the familiar correspondence between the importance of the objective and the appropriateness of the agency's role, along with the more widely spread evaluation of agency performance.

National policy on resource development—Developing a national policy that guides natural resource development of all kinds is another important objective (figure 10) for the respondents from Region 5 (mean 4.26), but the standard deviation of 1.12 indicates respondents are not all in agreement. Most respondents feel that the

Table 2--Other important objectives for Region 5 respondents.

OBJECTIVE:	Is this an important objective for you? (1=not at all important, 5=very important)	Do you believe that fulfilling this objective is an appropriate role for the USDA Forest Service? (1=strongly disagree, 5=strongly agree)	How favorably do you view the performance of the USDA Forest Service in fulfilling this objective? (1=very unfavorably, 5=very favorably)
Preserving the ability to have a 'wilderness' experience on forests and grasslands.	4.26 *1.00*[a] 109[b]	4.32 *1.02* 122	3.86 *1.17* 114
Informing the public on the potential environmental impacts of all uses associated with forests and grasslands.	4.24 *1.10* 87	4.51 *0.89* 91	3.22 *1.37* 82
Developing a national policy that guides natural resource development of all kinds (for example, specifies levels of extraction, and regulates environmental impacts).	4.26 *1.12* 113	4.16 *1.19* 79	3.36 *1.29* 95
Using public advisory committees to advise on public land management issues.	4.02 *1.14* 87	3.90 *1.05* 70	3.29 *1.12* 49
Encouraging collaboration between groups in order to share information concerning uses of forests and grasslands.	4.21 *1.15* 97	4.23 *1.05* 83	3.28 *1.21* 72
Preserving the natural resources of forests and grasslands through such policies as no timber harvesting or no mining.	4.09 *1.36* 101	4.17 *1.26* 109	3.57 *1.15* 90

[a] Standard deviation
[b] Sample size for each item (n) The sample sizes for each item are less than the full 636 sample since each respondent was asked only a portion of the 115 VOBA questions due to time limitations

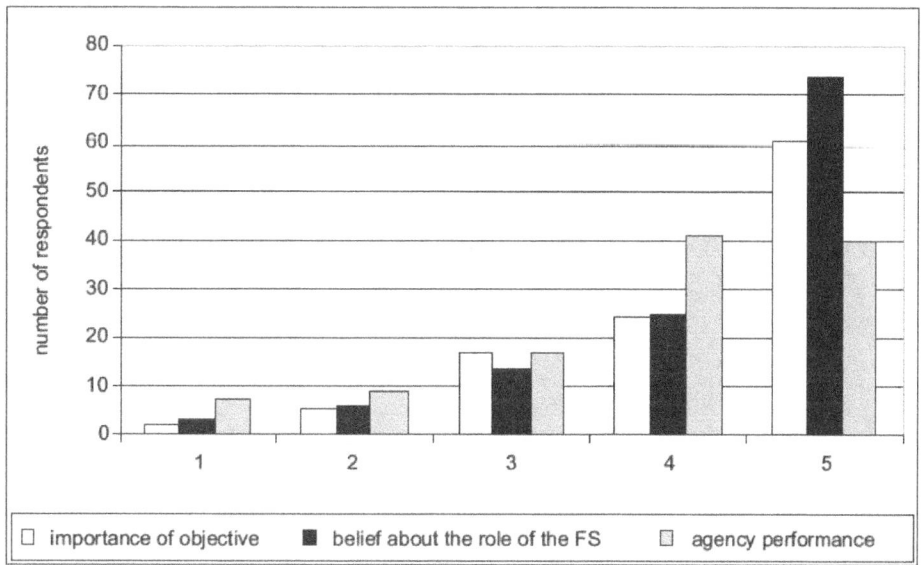

Figure 8—Distribution of Objectives, Beliefs, and Attitude scores for: Preserving the ability to have a "wilderness experience" on forests and grasslands.

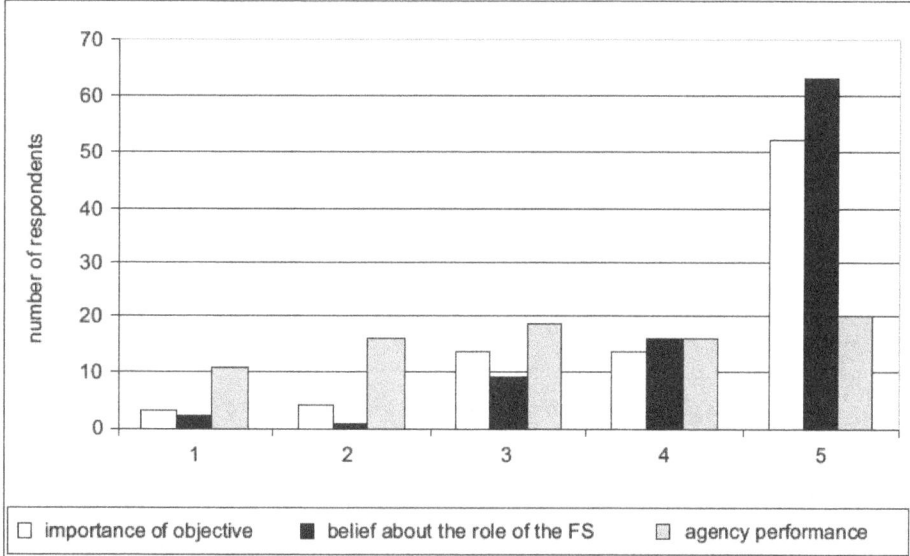

Figure 9—Distribution of Objectives, Beliefs, and Attitude scores for: Informing the public on the potential environmental impacts of all uses associated with forests and grasslands.

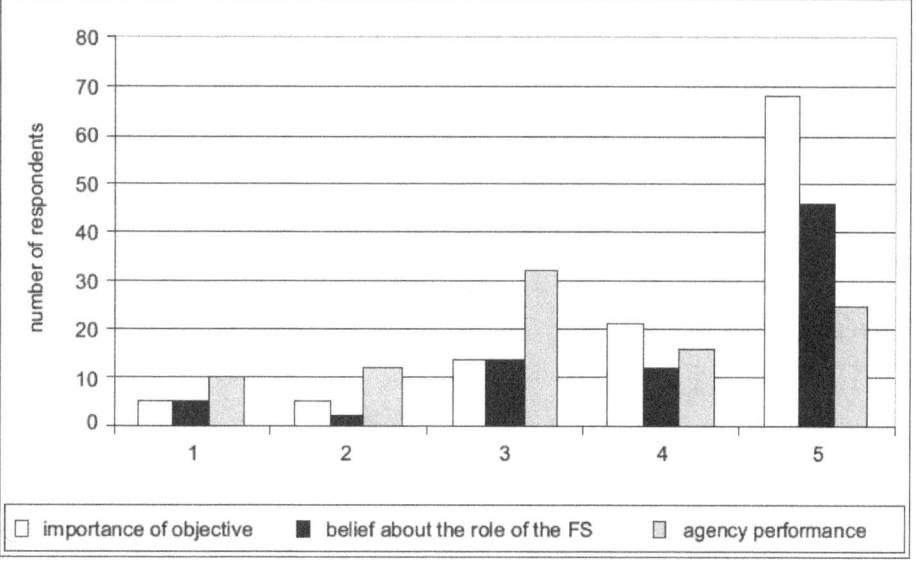

Figure 10—Distribution of Objectives, Beliefs, and Attitude scores for: Developing a national policy that guides natural resource development of all kinds (for example, specifies levels of extraction, and regulates environmental impacts).

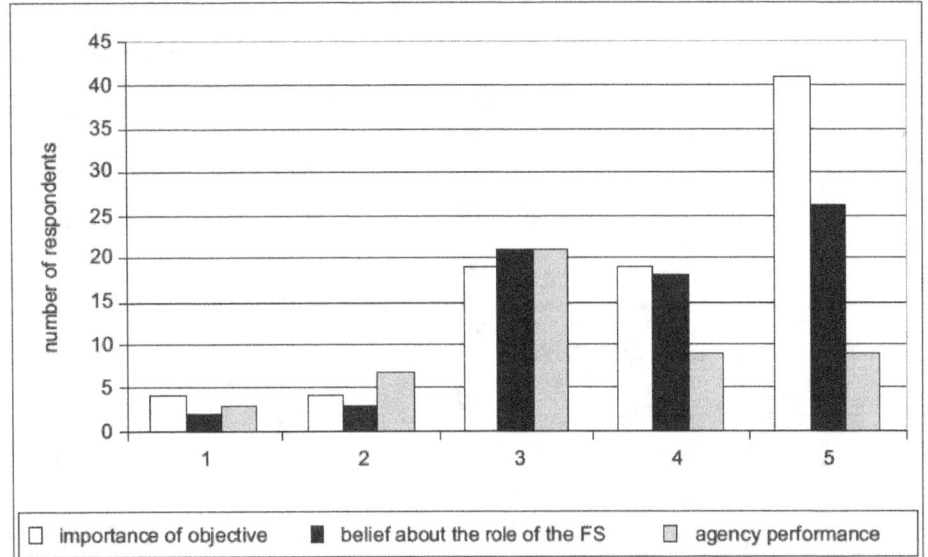

Figure 11—Distribution of Objectives, Beliefs, and Attitude scores for: Using public advisory committees to advise on public land management issues.

development of these programs is an appropriate role for the USDA Forest Service (mean 4.16, s.d. 1.19), and agency performance is seen as somewhat favorable (mean 3.36), although the standard deviation (1.29) again indicates a high level of disagreement.

Public advisory committees—Using public advisory committees to advise on public land management issues is important to the public from Region 5. The mean for this objective is 4.02, although the standard deviation (1.14) indicates some members do not hold this view. Respondents feel that the development of public advisory committees is a somewhat appropriate role for the agency (mean 3.90, s.d. 1.05). Agency performance on informing the public about these economic values is seen as favorable (mean 3.29), but again a high standard deviation (1.12) shows that this evaluation is not universal. Figure 11 shows the distribution of responses, illustrating the large percentage (63%) of respondents from Region 5 that view agency performance as neutral or unfavorable.

Encouraging collaboration—Encouraging collaboration between groups in order to share information concerning uses of forests and grasslands had a mean of 4.21. As with many of these important objectives, the somewhat high standard deviation (1.15) indicates that a number of respondents do not see this issue of encouraging collaboration as important. Responses from Region 5 reveal that the public views the encouragement of collaboration as an appropriate role for the agency (mean 4.23, s.d. 1.05). Finally, the USDA Forest Service is seen as doing a somewhat adequate job of encouraging

collaboration (mean 3.28), but again there is less than full consensus (s.d. 1.21). The histogram (figure 12) reveals that while the majority of the respondents view the objective as important and its fulfillment as an appropriate role for the agency, the distribution of opinions about agency performance is spread more evenly across the range of attitudes.

Preserving Forests and Grasslands through such policies as no timber harvesting or no mining—Although this objective has a mean of 4.09, the high standard deviation (1.36) may indicate there are also those in Region 5 who do not favor the elimination of timber harvesting or mining. The development of such national policies is seen as an appropriate role for the agency, although again a high level of disagreement exists (mean 4.17, s.d. 1.26). Likewise, agency performance is somewhat favorable (mean 3.57), but there is a low level of consensus on this performance (s.d. 1.15). Figure 13 illustrates the lack of consensus in the evaluation of agency performance, and shows that while most respondents agree that this objective is important and an appropriate role for the USDA Forest Service, there are also a good many that do not.

Objectives Identified as Not Important

Five objectives in the VOBA were identified as not important by the people of Region 5. While these objectives have a mean importance of less than 3.00 (3.00 is the midpoint of the scale, indicating a neutral position), all exhibit high standard deviations, indicating that

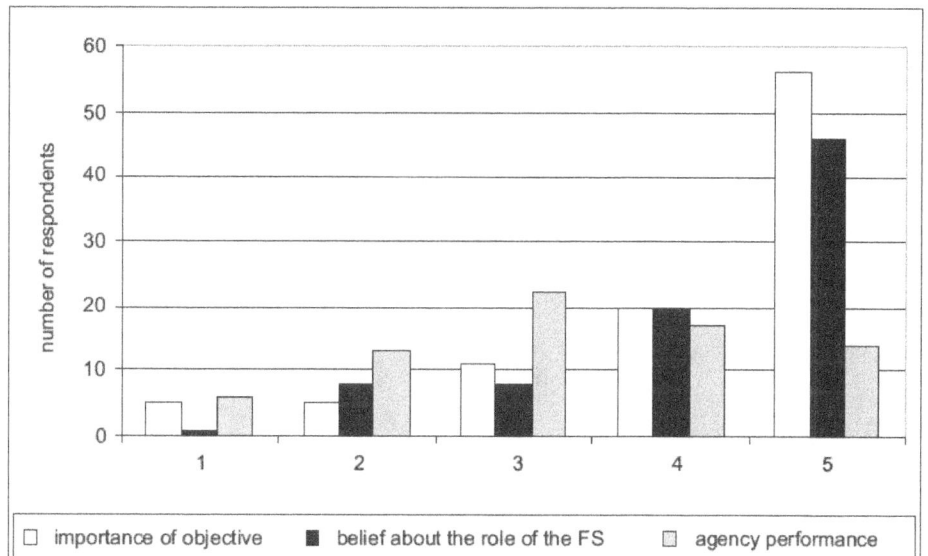

Figure 12—Distribution of Objectives, Beliefs, and Attitude scores for: Encouraging collaboration between groups in order to share information concerning uses of forests and grasslands.

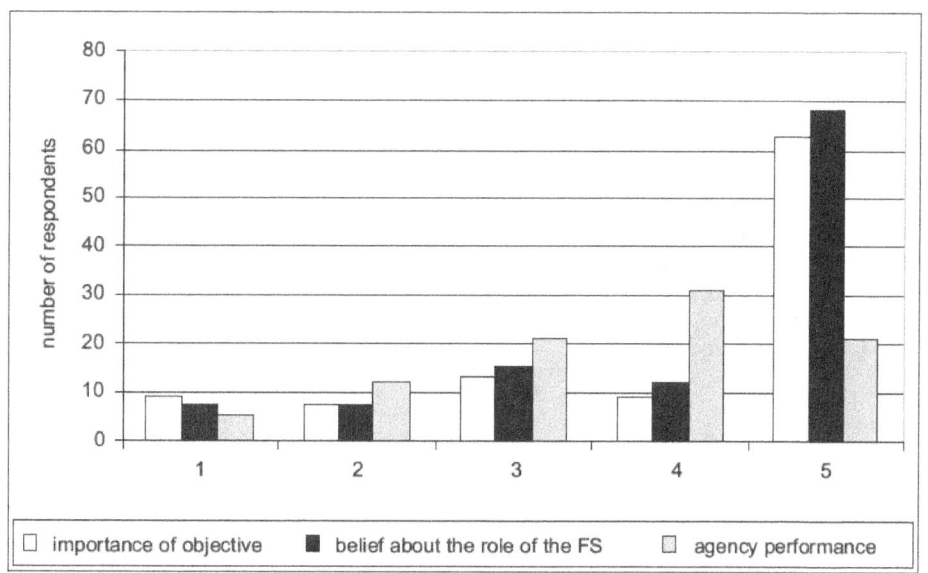

Figure 13—Distribution of Objectives, Beliefs, and Attitude scores for: Preserving the natural resources of forests and grasslands though such policies as no timber harvesting or no mining.

some respondents believe they are important. Divergent evaluations are not surprising since these objectives were included in the VOBA survey based upon the input of focus groups, some of which were comprised of specific stakeholder groups that may have had strong preferences for these objectives. In other words, while the general public does not feel that these objectives are important, there is a vocal minority that does. These less important objectives are presented in table 3.

Expanding off-highway motorized access—Although expanding motorized access is not important to most of the people of Region 5, there is little consensus for this

objective (mean 2.24, s.d. 1.41), indicating there is a constituency for whom such access is important. Overall, the public does not see the provision of such access as an appropriate role for the Forest Service (mean 2.37), although, again, the high standard deviation (1.45) indicates that there are many who do. Agency performance on the provision of off-highway motorized access is seen as slightly unfavorable (mean 2.97), but again this evaluation is not universal (s.d. 1.41). Figure 14 shows the distribution of these responses.

Developing paved roads—Developing new paved roads is also unimportant to most of the people of Region

Table 3--Distribution of Objectives, Beliefs, and Attitude scores for: Objectives that the Region 5 respondents do not view as important.

OBJECTIVE:	Is this an important objective for you? *(1=not at all important, 5=very important)*	Do you believe that fulfilling this objective is an appropriate role for the USDA Forest Service? *(1=strongly disagree, 5=strongly agree)*	How favorably do you view the performance of the USDA Forest Service in fulfilling this objective? *(1=very unfavorably, 5=very favorably)*
Expanding access for motorized off-highway vehicles on forests and grasslands (for example, snowmobiling or 4-wheel driving).	2.24 *1.41*[a] 93[b]	2.37 *1.45* 103	2.97 *1.41* 58
Developing new paved roads on forests and grasslands for access for cars and recreational vehicles.	2.32 *1.32* 96	2.45 *1.50* 99	3.23 *1.24* 78
Making the permitting process easier for some established uses of forests and grasslands such as grazing, logging, mining, and commercial recreation.	2.42 *1.39* 101	2.58 *1.36* 95	3.12 *1.35* 59
Developing and maintaining continuous trail systems that cross both public and private land for motorized vehicles such as snowmobiles or ATVs.	2.56 *1.41* 116	2.74 *1.36* 97	3.08 *1.32* 71
Expanding commercial recreation on forests and grasslands (for example, ski areas, guide services, or outfitters).	2.74 *1.35* 77	2.67 *1.40* 115	3.19 *1.26* 67

[a] Standard deviation
[b] Sample size for each item (n) The sample sizes for each item are less than the full 636 sample since each respondent was asked only a portion of the 115 VOBA questions due to time limitations

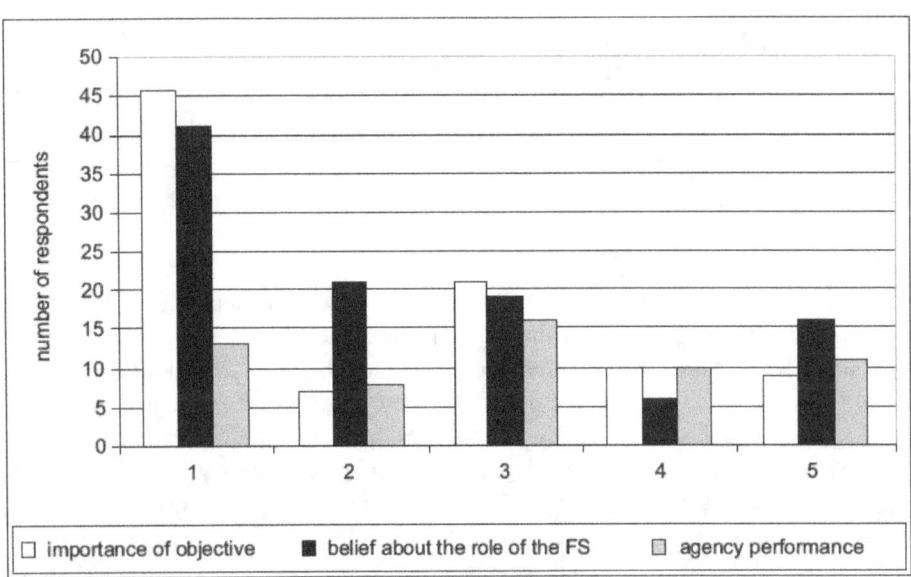

Figure 14—Distribution of Objectives, Beliefs, and Attitude scores for: Expanding access for motorized off-highway vehicles on forests and grasslands (for example, snowmobiling or 4-wheel driving).

USDA Forest Service RMRS-GTR-157. 2005.

5 (mean 2.32), but with evidence that there are also some for whom it is important (s.d. 1.32). Likewise, development of paved roads is not seen by most in Region 5 to be an appropriate role for the USDA Forest Service (mean 2.45), but there is a great deal of disagreement (s.d. 1.50). Finally, the USDA Forest Service is seen as doing a somewhat favorable job in developing new paved roads (mean 3.23), but as with the mean for the importance of this objective and for the belief about the role of the agency, there is little consensus for this evaluation (s.d. 1.24) (figure 15).

Easing the permitting process—Making the permitting process easier for some established uses (figure 16) is not viewed by most within the Region 5 public as an important objective (mean 2.42), but the high standard deviation (1.39) indicates some groups do view this as important. Making the permitting process easier is not seen as an appropriate role for the agency (mean 2.58). This assessment is not universally agreed upon, however, as indicated by a standard deviation of 1.36. The public in Region 5 views the performance of the Forest Service in easing the permitting process for some established

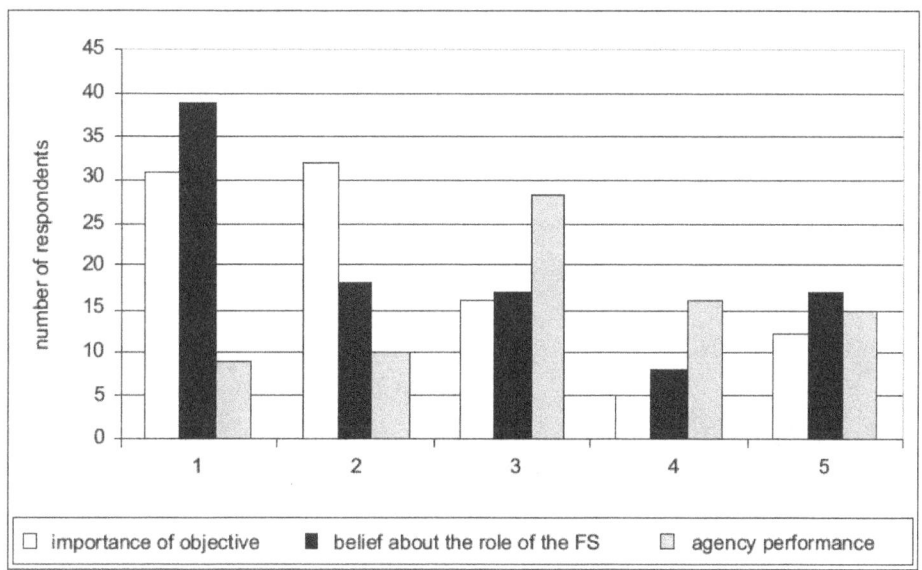

Figure 15—Distribution of Objectives, Beliefs, and Attitude scores for: Developing new paved roads on forests and grasslands for access for cars and recreational vehicles.

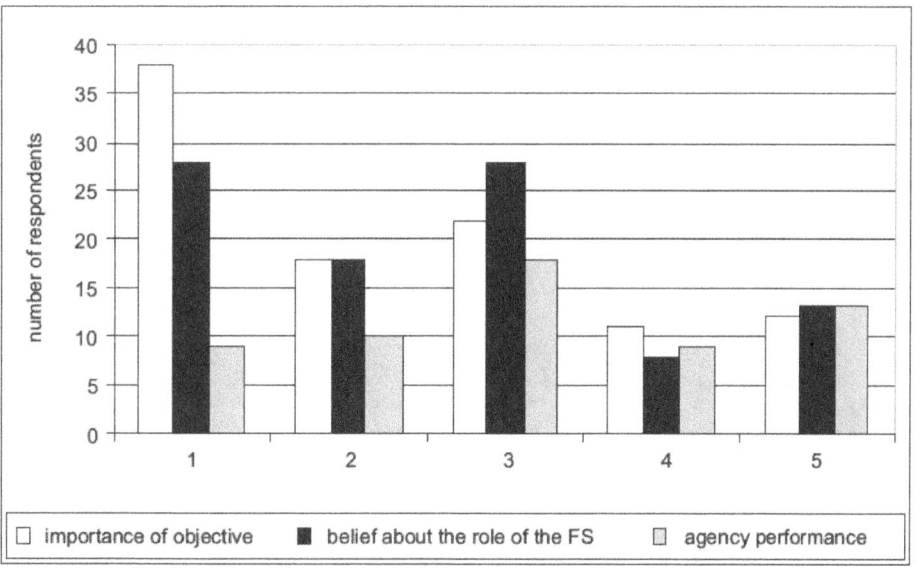

Figure 16—Distribution of Objectives, Beliefs, and Attitude scores for: Making the permitting process easier for some established uses of forests and grasslands such as grazing, logging, mining, and commercial recreation.

uses as somewhat favorable (mean 3.12), although there is some disagreement (s.d. 1.35).

Developing trail systems—The issue of developing and maintaining continuous trail systems that cross both public and private land for motorized vehicles such as snowmobiles or ATVs (figure 17) has a mean distribution of only 2.56, but the high standard deviation for this objective (1.41) indicates some groups may view this as an important objective. Likewise, developing and maintaining continuous trail systems is seen by most in Region 5 as a less than appropriate role for the USDA Forest Service (mean 2.74), but again there is little consensus (s.d. 1.36). Agency performance on the development and maintenance of continuous trail systems is seen as slightly favorable (mean 3.08), but, as with the other responses for this objective, this evaluation is not universal (s.d. 1.32).

Expanding commercial recreation—The issue of expanding commercial recreation on forests and grasslands (for example, ski areas, guide services, or outfitters) is not viewed as important by the respondents from Region 5 (mean 2.74), but the high standard deviation (1.35) again shows that there are also some for whom it is important. Expanding commercial recreation is often seen as a less than appropriate role for the USDA Forest Service (mean 2.67), although again, there is a lack of agreement (s.d. 1.40). Agency performance is slightly favorable (mean 3.19), but the standard deviation is 1.26, indicating that not all respondents agree. Figure 18 illustrates these evaluations.

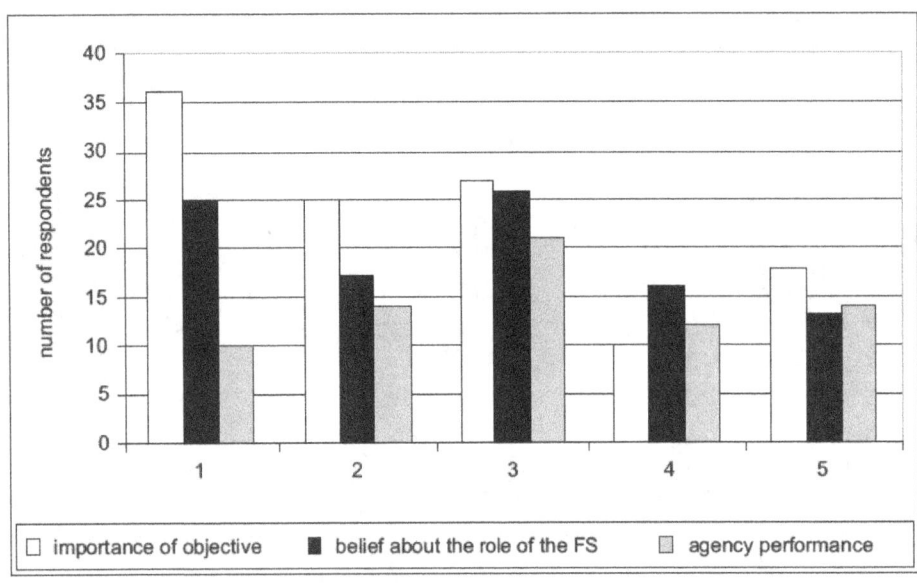

Figure 17—Distribution of Objectives, Beliefs, and Attitude scores for: Developing and maintaining continuous trail systems that cross both public and private land for motorized vehicles such as snowmobiles or ATVs.

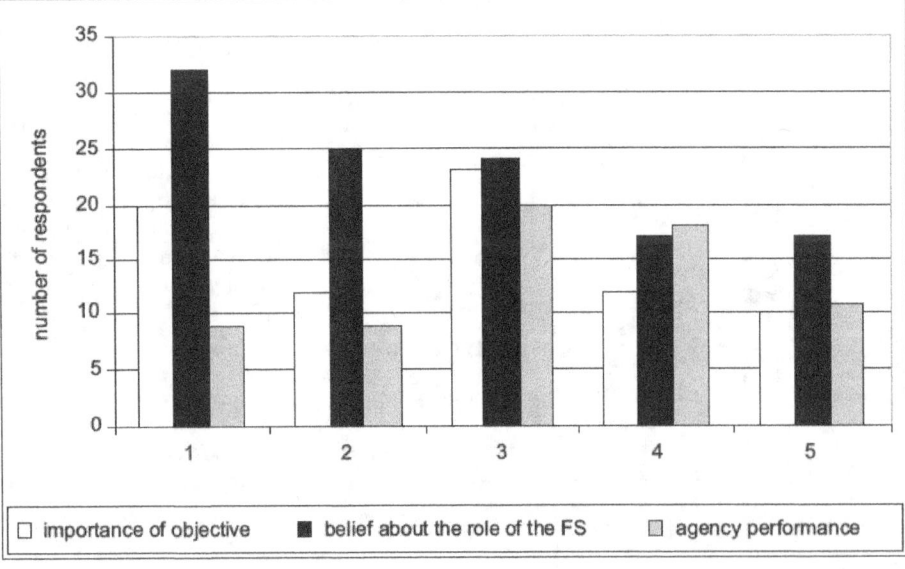

Figure 18—Distribution of Objectives, Beliefs, and Attitude scores for: Expanding commercial recreation on forests and grasslands (for example, ski areas, guide services, or outfitters).

Objectives Identified as Moderately Important

Table 4 presents the objectives the respondents from Region 5 feel are somewhat important, or those for which they are more neutral. Each objective within this set has a mean between 3.00 and 4.00. As with the less important objectives, all have relatively high standard deviations, indicating that while most people do not feel strongly about them, a few do. Results for this group of objectives have been organized by issue in table 4 (for example, objectives which deal either directly or indirectly with resource extraction are grouped together) to facilitate a discussion of related issues. Within these groupings, the objectives are organized in order of decreasing importance (those with higher means are listed first, then those with lower means).

Resource extraction and use—The first two objectives concerning resource extraction and use that are of moderate importance for the respondents from Region 5 deal with restriction of activities. For the restriction of mineral development on forests and grasslands, the distribution mean is 3.99 and the standard deviation is 1.20, showing a lack of consensus in the evaluation. The implementation of such restrictions are seen as a somewhat appropriate role for the USDA Forest Service (mean 3.81), although the high standard deviation (1.48) indicates many among the public disagree. Finally, the agency is doing a less than adequate job restricting timber harvesting and grazing, but again there is little consensus with this evaluation (mean 2.87, s.d. 1.34).

The restriction of timber harvesting and grazing on forests and grasslands (mean 3.83) also shows disagreement among the respondents from Region 5, as seen by the high standard deviation (1.33). The public of Region 5 feels that this type of restriction is an appropriate role for the USDA Forest Service (mean 4.26), although this is not a universally held evaluation (s.d. 1.48). Additionally, the respondents from Region 5 are favorable toward agency performance concerning the restriction of timber harvesting and grazing, although again with some disagreement (mean 3.20, s.d. 1.20).

Forests and grasslands have many cultural uses by Native Americans and Hispanics, and the preservation of these uses is seen as somewhat important by Region 5 respondents (mean 3.66). This opinion is not shared by all within the Region, as can be seen in the high standard deviation (1.39). Preserving such cultural uses is viewed as a somewhat important role for the USDA Forest Service (mean 3.41), but here again there is a lack of consensus for the evaluation (s.d. 1.40). Agency performance is somewhat favorable (mean 3.53), and there is more consensus with agency performance than with importance of the objective or appropriateness of the task for the Forest Service (s.d. 1.07).

Wilderness designation is often met with some controversy, and responses from Region 5 demonstrate this potential. While the mean for this objective indicates that most people feel it is somewhat important (3.58), the high standard deviation (1.47) also shows a high level of disagreement. The designation of wilderness is seen as an appropriate role for the agency (mean 3.69) although again this is not a universal opinion (s.d. 1.43). In this case the high standard deviation may actually reflect the knowledge that Congress, not the USDA Forest Service, is the body responsible for officially designating wilderness. The USDA Forest Service performance is viewed as somewhat favorable, but again there is a lack of consistency with this evaluation (mean 3.51, s.d. 1.11).

Many communities are dependent upon public forests and grasslands for their economic bases. Providing natural resources to these communities is a somewhat important objective for the people of Region 5 (mean 3.21). The importance of this objective is not universally agreed upon, however, as seen by the high standard deviation (1.35). The people of Region 5 see the agency role of providing natural resources to dependent communities as somewhat appropriate (mean 3.02), but again there is little consensus (s.d. 1.44). Finally, agency performance in providing these natural resources is rated as somewhat favorable (mean 3.31), although there is disagreement (s.d. 1.19).

Public relations and management—Region 5 respondents feel that informing the public on the economic value received by developing our natural resources is a moderately important objective (mean 3.94). However, there is some disagreement with this assessment (s.d. 1.34). Many of these respondents feel that the Forest Service should be informing the public on economic values (mean 3.54), although not all respondents agreed with this (s.d. 1.38). Agency performance is somewhat favorable (mean 3.08), but again with a lack of consensus for this evaluation (s.d. 1.29).

Making management decisions at the local level rather than at the national level is always important to at least some stakeholders. The people of Region 5 find the making of management decisions concerning the use of forests and grasslands at the local level a moderately important objective (mean 3.78, s.d. 1.16). Local

Table 4--Objectives of moderate importance for Region 5 respondents.

OBJECTIVE:		Is this an important objective for you? *(1=not at all important, 5=very important)*	Do you believe that fulfilling this objective is an appropriate role for the USDA Forest Service? *(1=strongly disagree, 5=strongly agree)*	How favorably do you view the performance of the USDA Forest Service in fulfilling this objective? *(1=very unfavorably, 5=very favorably)*
Resource Extraction and Use	Restricting mineral development on forests and grasslands.	3.99 *1.20[a]* 88 [b]	3.81 *1.48* 102	2.87 *1.34* 67
	Restricting timber harvesting and grazing on forests and grasslands.	3.83 *1.33* 94	4.26 *1.08* 91	3.20 *1.20* 79
	Preserving the cultural uses of forests and grasslands by Native Americans and Native Hispanics[#] such as firewood gathering, herb/berry/plant gathering, and ceremonial uses.	3.66 *1.39* 129	3.41 *1.40* 107	3.53 *1.07* 83
	Designating more wilderness areas on public land that stops access for development and motorized uses.	3.58 *1.47* 77	3.69 *1.43* 102	3.51 *1.11* 75
	Providing natural resources from forests and grasslands to support communities dependent on grazing, mining, or timber harvesting.	3.21 *1.35* 89	3.02 *1.44* 82	3.31 *1.19* 89
Public Relations & Management	Informing the public on the economic value received by developing our natural resources.	3.94 *1.34* 99	3.54 *1.38* 96	3.08 *1.29* 77
	Making management decisions concerning the use of forests and grasslands at the local level rather than at the national level.	3.78 *1.16* 73	3.74 *1.31* 90	3.18 *1.23* 68
Recreation	Developing and maintaining continuous trail systems that cross both public and private land for non-motorized recreation such as hiking or cross-country skiing.	3.82 *1.24* 100	3.72 *1.25* 83	3.48 *1.07* 61
	Increasing law enforcement efforts by public land agencies on public lands.	3.73 *1.29* 79	3.90 *1.24* 92	3.69 *1.14* 68
	Designating some existing trails for specific use (for example, creating separate trails for snowmobiling and cross-country skiing or for mountain biking and horseback riding.)	3.51 *1.30* 88	3.78 *1.17* 88	3.48 *1.14* 85
	Paying an entry fee that goes to support public land	3.38 *1.43* 79	3.71 *1.27* 89	3.57 *1.30* 76
Land Acquisition	Increasing the total number of acres in the public land system.	3.69 *1.42* 68	4.09 *1.27* 70	3.29 *1.37* 68
	Allowing public land mangers to trade public lands for private lands (for example, to eliminate private property within public land boundaries, or to acquire unique areas of land).	3.26 *1.40* 68	3.43 *1.36* 74	3.02 *1.18* 55

[a] Standard deviation
[b] Sample size for each item (n) The sample sizes for each item are less than the full 636 sample since each respondent was asked only a portion of the 115 VOBA questions due to time limitations
[#] The term "Native Hispanic" was used in the survey to differentiate Hispanics born in the US from those who moved to the US This term was changed to "traditional groups" in the 2003 survey

USDA Forest Service RMRS-GTR-157. 2005.

decision-making is viewed by Region 5 residents to be an appropriate role for the agency, although there is a lack of consensus (mean 3.74, s.d. 1.31). The performance of the USDA Forest Service is viewed somewhat favorably (mean 3.18, s.d. 1.23).

Recreation—The development of continuous trail systems, crossing both public and private land, for non-motorized access is seen as somewhat important (mean 3.82, s.d. 1.24). This may indicate that while many people would like to have access to this type of system, there are also many respondents (potentially affected landowners) who would see it as an infringement of property rights. Interestingly, the residents of Region 5 do not find the development of a similar trail system for motorized recreation to be important (see "Objectives Identified as Not Important by Respondents in Region 5"). The development of a system of private/public non-motorized access is viewed as a somewhat appropriate role for the agency (mean 3.72), however again with a level of disagreement (s.d. 1.25). Agency performance is evaluated as somewhat favorable, but, as with the other aspects of this objective, this evaluation is not universally held (mean 3.48, s.d. 1.07).

Law enforcement on public lands is moderately important to Region 5 residents, although some lack of agreement exists (mean 3.73, s.d. 1.29). Respondents in Region 5 believe that increasing law enforcement is a somewhat appropriate role for the USDA Forest Service, but again there is considerable disagreement with the evaluation (mean 3.90, s.d. 1.24). Agency performance is viewed as favorable by many Region 5 residents, but again there is a lack of consensus for this evaluation (mean 3.69, s.d. 1.14).

Conflicts between incompatible recreation uses are often an issue on public lands, including those in the National Forest System. One solution to this type of conflict is to designate some trails for specific uses (for example separate trails for cross-country skiing and snowmobiling). When asked about designating trails for specific uses, respondents from Region 5 reported that it is somewhat important, with some disagreement (mean 3.51, s.d. 1.30). Region 5 residents believe creating such designations for trails is an appropriate role for the Forest Service (mean 3.78, s.d. 1.17) and gave the agency a somewhat favorable performance evaluation (mean 3.48, s.d. 1.14).

Most respondents in Region 5 feel that it is somewhat important to pay an entry fee to support public lands

(mean 3.38), but as can be expected, there is a lack of consensus on this objective (s.d. 1.43). The people of Region 5 feel this would be an appropriate role for the agency, but again, there is disagreement (mean 3.71, 1.27). Finally, agency performance is seen as adequate, although there is a lack of consensus (mean 3.57, s.d. 1.30).

Land acquisition—Increasing the total number of acres in the public land system is seen by respondents from Region 5 as a somewhat important objective (mean 3.69). This is revealed as a potentially contentious issue due to the evident lack of consensus (s.d. 1.42). The people of Region 5 see adding to the public domain as a highly appropriate role for the agency (mean 4.09), but lack of agreement about this assessment (s.d. 1.27) may indicate differences in knowledge about who would actually have the authority to acquire additional public lands. Overall, respondents from Region 5 gave the Forest Service a somewhat adequate rating (mean 3.29), although not everyone agrees (s.d. 1.37).

Finally, although allowing public land managers to trade public lands for private lands is a somewhat important objective for Region 5 residents, this objective is far from universally supported (mean 3.26, s.d. 1.40). The USDA Forest Service is generally viewed as an appropriate agency to fulfill this objective, although not all groups view it as such (mean 3.43, s.d. 1.36). Agency performance is seen as somewhat favorable, with a mean of 3.02 and standard deviation of 1.18.

Results for Region 5: Public Lands Values_____

Previous research using the Public Lands Values Scale has shown that these items consistently fall into two categories. The first category, which deals with individual actions or values, has been labeled Socially Responsible Individual Values (tables 5 and 6). For these values, a higher mean indicates a higher level of environmental orientation. The second category, which deals with how public lands should be managed, has been labeled Socially Responsible Management Values (table 7). These values statements are worded so that a higher value indicates that relatively more importance is placed upon human uses of, or commodity production from, forests and grasslands.

Table 5--Socially responsible individual public lands values for Region 5 with a high level of agreement among respondents.

Values *(1=strongly disagree. 5=strongly agree)*	Mean
Manufacturers should be encouraged to use recycled materials in their manufacturing and processing operations.	4.76 *0.69*[a] 157[b]
People should be more concerned about how our public lands are used.	4.67 *0.76* 141
I am willing to make personal sacrifices for the sake of slowing down pollution.	4.53 *0.78* 155
Future generations should be as important as the current one in the decisions about public lands.	4.54 *0.91* 170
Donating time or money to worthy causes is important to me.	4.38 *0.91* 147
Consumers should be interested in the environmental consequences of the products they purchase.	4.48 *0.93* 146
I am glad there are National Forests even if I never get to see them.	4.64 *0.94* 181

[a] Standard deviation
[b] Sample size for each item (n). The sample sizes for each item are less than the full 636 sample since each respondent was asked only a portion of the 115 VOBA questions due to time limitations.

Socially Responsible Individual Values

Most of the means for the values in tables 5 and 6 indicate an environmental orientation in the people of Region 5. For many of the values statements, however, the standard deviation indicates a low level of agreement. Therefore, responses to the Socially Responsible Individual Values are broken into two groups, those for which there is a high degree of consensus and those for which the level of agreement is lower (based upon the standard deviation).

Socially Responsible Individual Values With a High Degree of Consensus

It is interesting to note (table 5) that when Socially Responsible Individual Values with a higher degree of agreement (standard deviation of 1.00 or less) are placed in order of increasing standard deviation, the general order of the mean scores decreases. In other words, the values statements with higher means (indicating more environmentally oriented values) are also those with higher levels of consensus.

Socially Responsible Individual Values With a Low Degree of Consensus

Table 6 shows the values statements with lower consensus among the respondents. These again nearly always exhibit the characteristic that higher levels of environmental orientation also correspond to higher consensus (even among these values with low consensus).

Figure 19 shows the responses to the statement "I would be willing to pay $5 more each time I use public lands for recreational purposes." While many respondents agree with this statement (mean 3.47), there is a noticeable amount of disagreement indicated by the high standard deviation (1.53). The figure shows that there is an identifiable minority who clearly disagrees. Since fees are often a reality in order to provide such recreation opportunities, it is important to be aware that although

Table 6--Socially responsible individual public lands values for Region 5 with a low level of agreement among respondents.

Values (1=strongly disagree, 5=strongly agree)	Mean
I am willing to stop buying products from companies that pollute the environment even though it might be inconvenient.	4.10 *1.06* [a] 147 [b]
People can think public lands are valuable even if they never go there themselves.	4.42 *1.07* 137
Forests have a right to exist for their own sake, regardless of human concerns and uses.	4.30 *1.09* 175
People should urge their friends to limit their use of products made from scarce resources.	4.06 *1.16* 171
I have often thought that if we could just get by with a little less there would be more left for future generations.	4.12 *1.17* 137
The whole pollution issue has never upset me too much since I feel it's somewhat overrated. [c]	3.00 *1.24* 162
I would be willing to sign a petition for an environmental cause.	3.97 *1.30* 152
Wildlife, plants, and humans have equal rights to live and grow.	4.06 *1.34* 133
Natural resources should be preserved even if people must do without some products.	4.18 *1.41* 150
I would be willing to pay five dollars more each time I use public lands for recreational purposes (for example, hiking, camping, hunting).	3.47 *1.53* 156

[a] Standard deviation

[b] Sample size for each item (n). The sample sizes for each item are less than the full 636 sample since each respondent was asked only a portion of the 115 VOBA questions due to time limitations.

[c] This value statement has been reverse scored to make the responses consistent with the other statements. For a more complete discussion of reverse scoring, please refer to the appendix.

most people support them, such policies will most likely be met with some level of resistance.

Socially Responsible Management Values

The results for the Socially Responsible Management Values (table 7) are presented in order from higher agreement to lower agreement. As the previous section demonstrates, although most people believe in protecting the environment, disagreement arises about the appropriate methods to achieve such protection. The differences in responses to this set of values are likely the basis for disagreement noted in some of the aforementioned objectives. Histograms are presented for each Socially

Responsible Management Values, but only the first is discussed because of its direct relevance to customer satisfaction.

It is interesting to note the low level of agreement with the statement "The government has better places to spend money than devoting resources to a strong conservation program." Furthermore, although there is a relatively high level of disagreement among the respondents in Region 5 regarding this statement, there is more agreement for this statement than any of the other Socially Responsible Management Public Lands Values. Figure 20 shows the distribution of responses to this statement. Figures 21 through 27 show distribution of responses to the other seven "Management Values" statements.

Table 7--Socially responsible management public lands values for Region 5.

Values *(1=strongly disagree. 5=strongly agree)*	Mean
The government has better places to spend money than devoting resources to a strong conservation program.	1.93 *1.15*[a] 194[b]
I think that the public land managers are doing an adequate job of protecting natural resources from being overused.	3.01 *1.25* 158
The Federal government should subsidize the development and leasing of public lands to companies.	2.03 *1.30* 195
The decision to develop resources should be based mostly on economic grounds.	2.42 *1.33* 179
The most important role for the public lands is providing jobs and income for local people.	2.90 *1.46* 210
The primary use of forests should be for products that are useful to humans.	2.64 *1.46* 209
The main reason for maintaining resources today is so we can use them in the future if we need to.	3.58 *1.48* 183
We should actively harvest more trees to meet the needs of a much larger human population.	2.49 *1.51* 203

[a] Standard deviation
[b] Sample size for each item (n). The sample sizes for each item are less than the full 636 sample since each respondent was asked only a portion of the 115 VOBA questions due to time limitations.

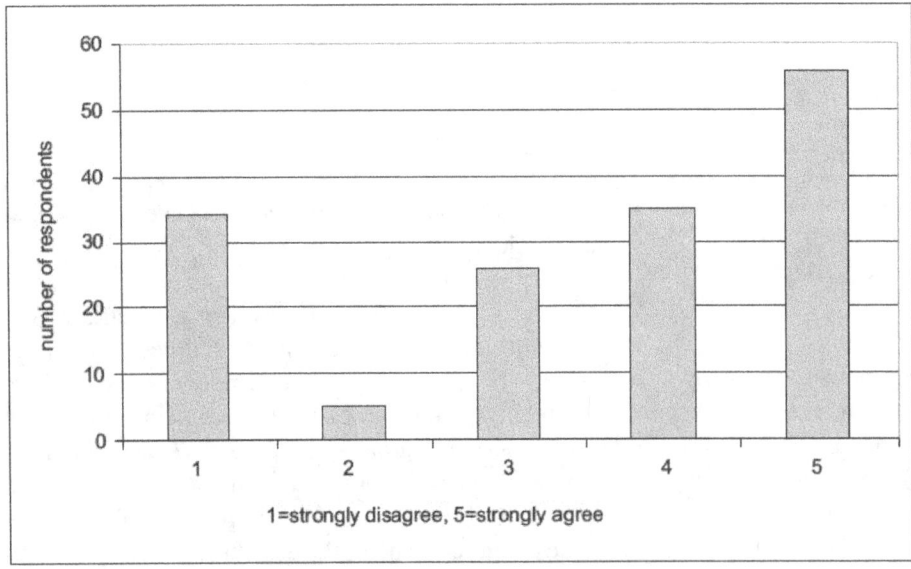

Figure 19—Distribution of responses to: "I would be willing to pay five dollars more each time I use public lands for recreational purposes (for example, hiking, camping, hunting)."

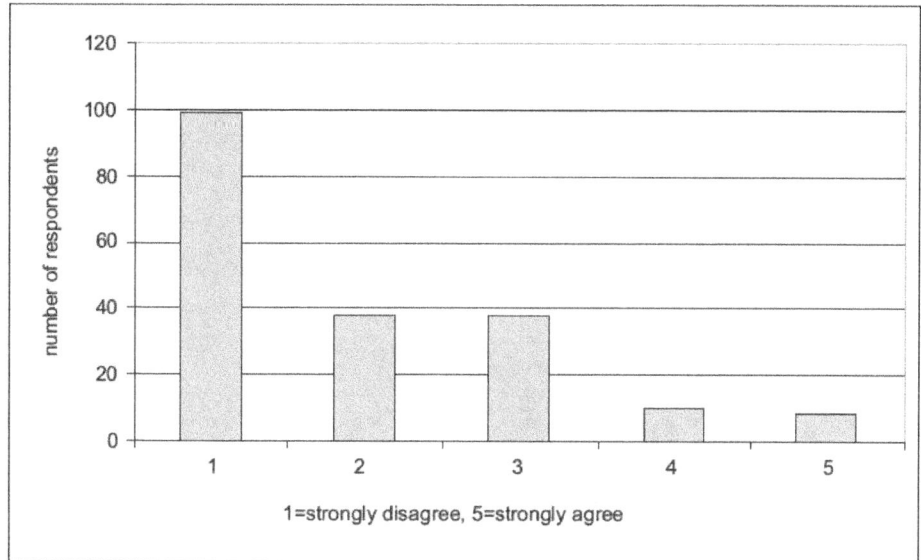

Figure 20—Distribution of responses to: "The government has better places to spend money than devoting resources to a strong conservation program."

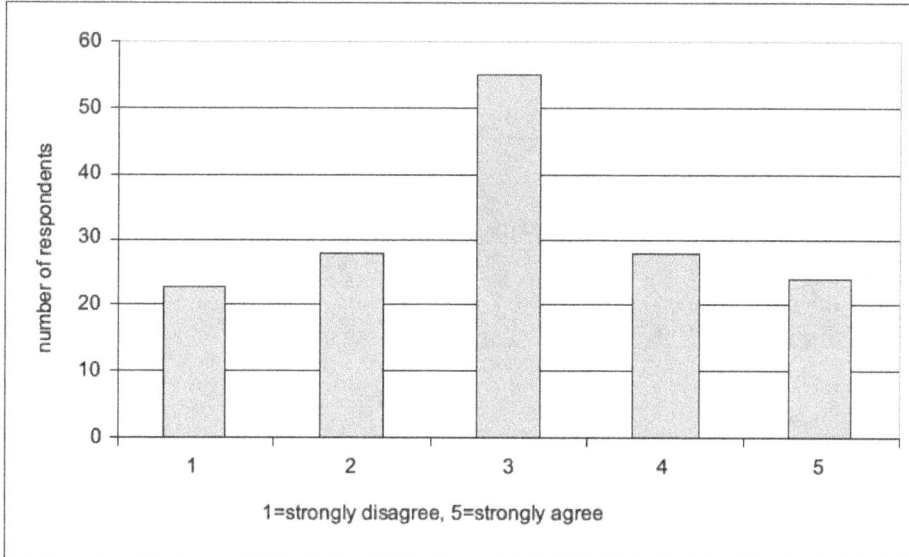

Figure 21—Distribution of responses to: "I think that the public land managers are doing an adequate job of protecting natural resources from being overused."

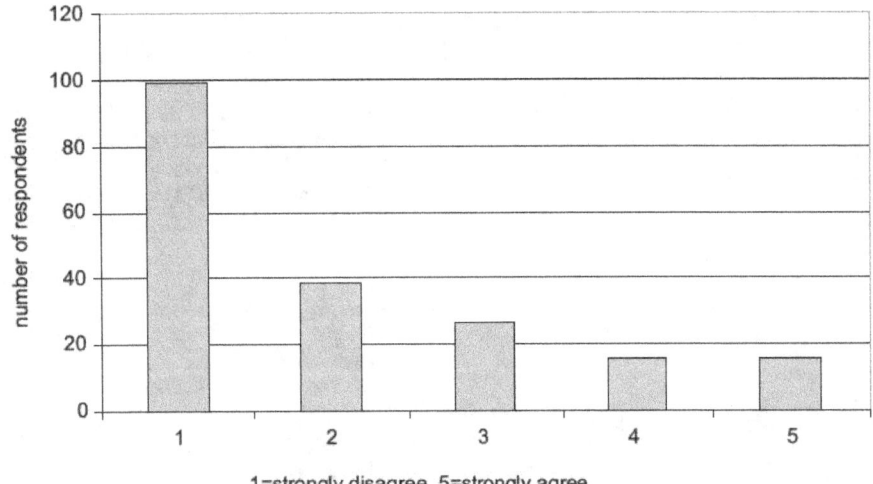

Figure 22—Distribution of responses to: "The Federal government should subsidize the development and leasing of public lands to companies."

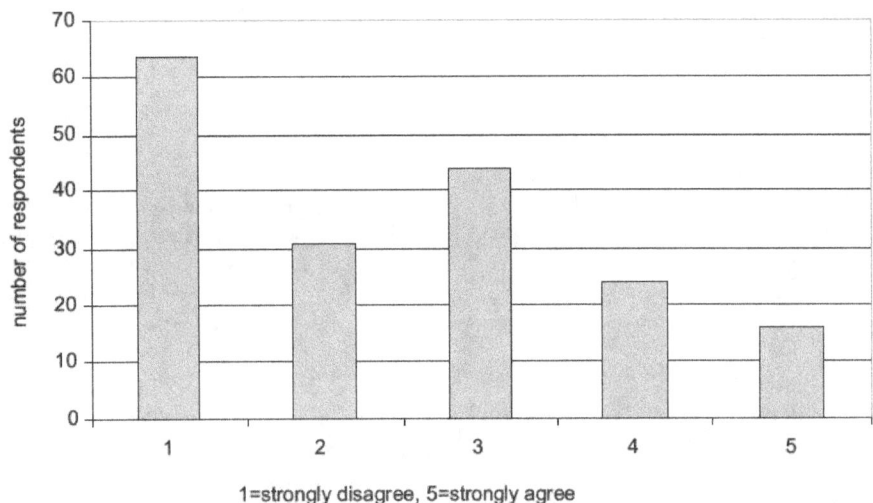

Figure 23—Distribution of responses to: "The decision to develop resources should be based mostly on economic grounds."

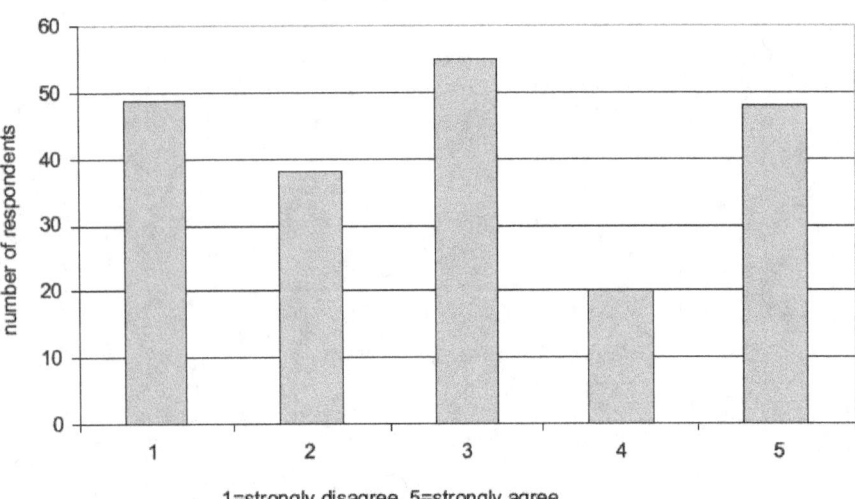

Figure 24—Distribution of responses to: "The most important role for the public lands is providing jobs and income for local people."

USDA Forest Service RMRS-GTR-157. 2005.

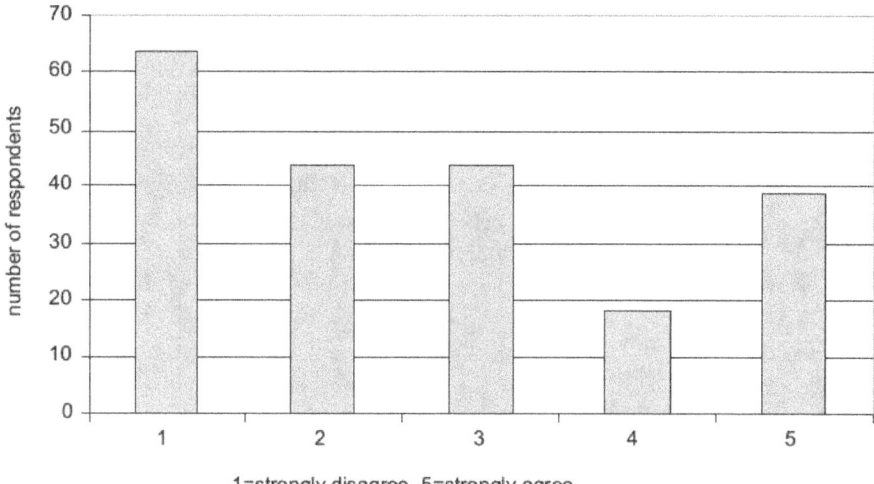

Figure 25—Distribution of responses to: "The primary use of forests should be for products that are useful to humans."

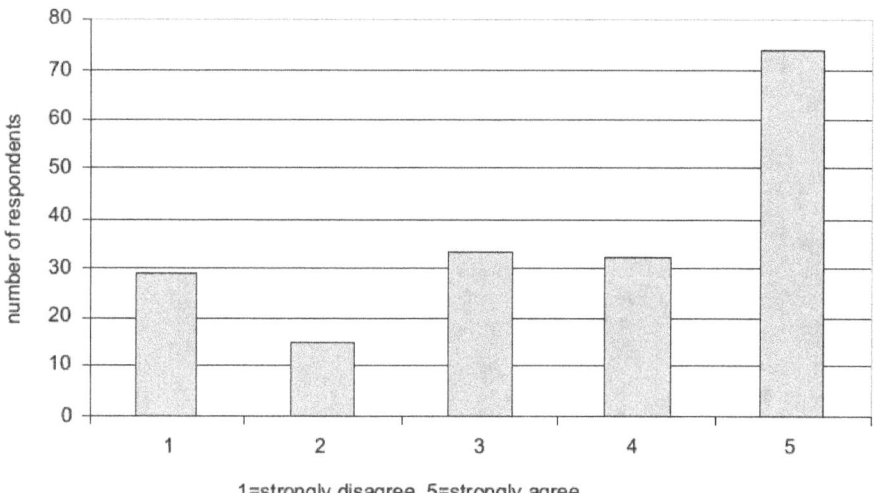

Figure 26—Distribution of responses to: "The main reason for maintaining resources today is so we can use them in the future if we need to."

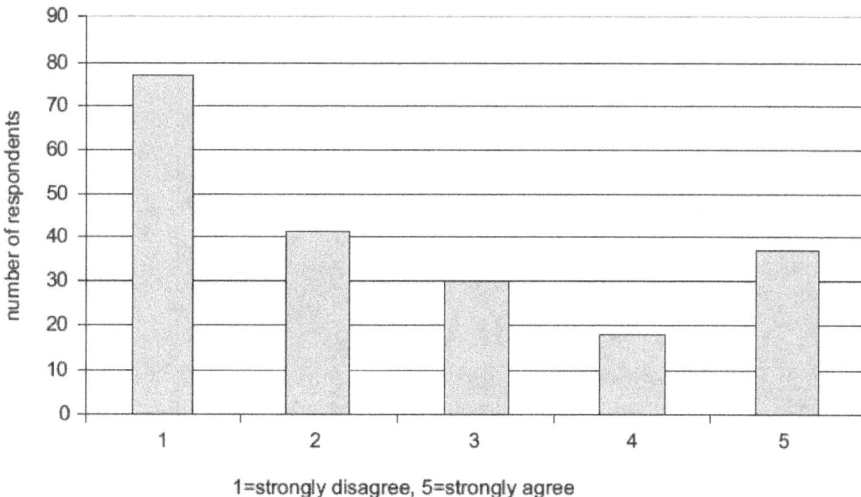

Figure 27—Distribution of responses to: "We should actively harvest more trees to meet the needs of a much larger human population.

Comparison of Region 5 With the Rest of the United States_____

The final section of this report compares the VOBA results for Region 5 with the results for the rest of the United States. Tables 8 through 11 present the objectives, beliefs about the role of the agency, and customer satisfaction. These are arranged into the same groups as in the sections above (Core Important Objectives, Other Important Objectives, Unimportant Objectives, and Objectives of Moderate Importance). Tables 12 and 13 contain the comparison for the Public Lands Values. These are arranged into Socially Responsible Individual Values and Socially Responsible Management Values. Discussion focuses on those objectives and values with statistically significant differences.

Objectives Identified as Important

Core Important Objectives

Region 5 does not significantly differ from the rest of the United States regarding the importance for any of the core objectives. Region 5 does believe more strongly, however, that protecting ecosystems and wildlife habitats is an appropriate role for the USDA Forest Service than does the rest of the United States (mean for Region 5, 4.74, for the rest of the United States, 4.54). There is substantial agreement about this evaluation within both Region 5 and the rest of the United States, although Region 5 does show greater agreement (standard deviation for Region 5, 0.67, for the rest of the United States 0.90). Table 8 shows the variation between Region 5 and the rest of the United States for the core objectives.

Other Important Objectives

Within the category of other important objectives, evaluations of the respondents from Region 5 match

Table 8--Comparison of core important objectives, beliefs, and attitudes between Region 5 and the rest of the United States.

OBJECTIVE	Is this an important objective for you? (1=not at all important, 5=very important)		Sig. diff –R5/rest US	Do you believe that fulfilling this objective is an appropriate role for the USDA Forest Service? (1=strongly disagree, 5=strongly agree)		Sig. diff -R5/rest US	How favorably do you view the performance of the USDA Forest Service in fulfilling this objective? (1=very unfavorably, 5=very favorably)		Sig. diff - R5/ rest US
	Region 5	Rest of US		Region 5	Rest of US		Region 5	Rest of US	
Conserving and protecting forests and grasslands that are the source of our water resources, such as streams, lakes, and watershed areas.	4.68 0.85[a] 95[b]	4.72 0.75 1232		4.66 0.77 120	4.59 0.84 1286		3.75 1.09 113	3.84 1.10 1081	
Informing the public about recreation concerns on forests and grasslands such as safety, trail etiquette, and respect for wildlife.	4.65 0.74 89	4.53 0.90 1078		4.44 0.98 106	4.52 0.90 1048		3.79 1.24 111	3.88 1.17 1139	
Protecting ecosystems and wildlife habitats.	4.61 0.77 132	4.55 0.92 1390		4.74 0.67 112	4.54 0.90 1210	**	3.79 1.02 110	3.86 1.11 1148	
Developing volunteer programs to improve forests and grasslands (for example, planting trees, or improving water quality).	4.56 0.93 118	4.54 0.86 1177		4.51 0.91 102	4.51 0.92 1222		3.56 1.23 77	3.73 1.18 878	
Developing volunteer programs to maintain trails and facilities on forests and grasslands (for example, trail maintenance or campground maintenance).	4.24 0.97 85	4.15 1.05 1022		4.40 0.87 91	4.18 1.05 1074		3.68 1.28 80	3.72 1.12 877	
Allowing for diverse uses of forests and grasslands such as grazing, recreation, and wildlife habitat.	4.03 0.98 94	4.05 1.10 1036		4.07 1.21 75	4.05 1.12 884		3.66 1.08 58	3.67 1.08 791	

[a] Standard deviation
[b] Sample size for each item (n).
*, **, *** mean differences are statistically significant at $\alpha = 0.05$, 0.01, and 0.001 respectively, based on a t-test.

those of the rest of the United States with one minor variation. Respondents from Region 5 view the performance of the USDA Forest Service in encouraging collaboration less favorably then do respondents from the rest of the United States (mean for Region 5, 3.28, mean for the rest of the United States, 3.59). Not surprising, Region 5 respondents' less favorable evaluation is coupled with greater disagreement than the more favorable evaluation from respondents in the rest of the United States (s.d. for Region 5, 1.21, s.d. for the rest of the United States, 1.13). Table 9 shows the variation between the respondents from Region 5 and those from the rest of the United States for the important objectives.

Objectives Identified as Not Important

Respondents from Region 5 evaluated the objective of making the permitting process easier for some established uses of forests and grasslands such as grazing, logging, mining, and commercial recreation as even less important than respondents from the rest of the United States (mean for Region 5, 2.42, mean for the rest of the United States, 2.77). Consistency of evaluation was nearly the same for both groups of respondents.

There is again only one statistically significant difference between the views of the respondents from Region 5 and the views of the respondents from the rest of the United States in evaluating appropriateness roles for the USDA Forest Service. Region 5 evaluated the expansion of commercial recreation to be less appropriate than did respondents from the rest of the United States (mean for Region 5, 2.67, mean for the rest of the United States, 3.05). There was also less agreement about this evaluation for Region 5 respondents (s.d. for Region 5, 1.40, s.d. for the rest of the United States, 1.35).

Finally, the comparison of Region 5 respondents' evaluation of the USDA Forest Service performance with the evaluation from respondents from the rest of the United States reveals there are no statistically significant differences. Table 10 shows the comparison for objectives evaluated to be less than important.

Table 9--Comparison of other important objectives, beliefs, and attitudes between Region 5 and the rest of the United States.

OBJECTIVE	Is this an important objective for you? (1=not at all important, 5=very important)			Do you believe that fulfilling this objective is an appropriate role for the USDA Forest Service? (1=strongly disagree, 5=strongly agree)			How favorably do you view the performance of the USDA Forest Service in fulfilling this objective? (1=very unfavorably, 5=very favorably)		
	Region 5	Rest of US	Sig. diff –R5/rest US	Region 5	Rest of US	Sig. diff –R5/rest US	Region 5	Rest of US	Sig. diff –R5/rest US
Preserving the ability to have a wilderness experience on forests and grasslands.	4.26 / 1.00[a] / 109[b]	4.22 / 1.11 / 1232		4.32 / 1.02 / 122	4.21 / 1.10 / 1237		3.86 / 1.17 / 114	3.86 / 1.01 / 1287	
Informing the public on the potential environmental impacts of all uses associated with forests and grasslands.	4.24 / 1.10 / 87	4.40 / 0.98 / 1085		4.51 / 0.89 / 91	4.44 / 0.94 / 1044		3.22 / 1.37 / 82	3.43 / 1.26 / 931	
Developing a national policy that guides natural resource development of all kinds (for example, specifies levels of extraction and regulates environmental impacts).	4.26 / 1.12 / 113	4.22 / 1.17 / 1182		4.16 / 1.19 / 79	4.15 / 1.15 / 1029		3.36 / 1.29 / 95	3.44 / 1.22 / 898	
Using public advisory committees to advise on public land management issues.	4.02 / 1.14 / 87	3.83 / 1.16 / 883		3.90 / 1.05 / 70	3.88 / 1.16 / 857		3.29 / 1.12 / 49	3.32 / 1.19 / 671	
Encouraging collaboration between groups in order to share information concerning uses of forests and grasslands.	4.21 / 1.15 / 97	4.21 / 1.08 / 969		4.23 / 1.05 / 83	4.19 / 1.04 / 984		3.28 / 1.21 / 72	3.59 / 1.13 / 829	**
Preserving the natural resources of forests and grasslands through such policies as no timber harvesting or not mining.	4.09 / 1.36 / 101	4.15 / 1.21 / 1258		4.17 / 1.26 / 109	4.12 / 1.26 / 1234		3.57 / 1.15 / 90	3.60 / 1.24 / 1079	

[a] Standard deviation
[b] Sample size for each item (n).
*, **, *** mean differences are statistically significant at α = 0.05, 0.01, and 0.001 respectively, based on a t-test.

Table 10--Comparison of the objectives, beliefs, and attitudes identified as not important by Region 5 with the rest of the United States.

OBJECTIVE	Is this an important objective for you? *(1=not at all important, 5=very important)*			Do you believe that fulfilling this objective is an appropriate role for the USDA Forest Service? *(1=strongly disagree, 5=strongly agree)*			How favorably do you view the performance of the USDA Forest Service in fulfilling this objective? *(1=very unfavorably, 5=very favorably)*		
	Region 5	Rest of US	Sig. diff –R5/rest US	Region 5	Rest of US	Sig. diff –R5/rest US	Region 5	Rest of US	Sig. diff –R5/rest US
Expanding access for motorized off-highway vehicles on forests and grasslands (for example, snowmobiling or 4-wheel driving).	2.24 *1.41[a]* 93[b]	2.27 *1.40* 1036		2.37 *1.45* 103	2.42 *1.37* 1169		2.97 *1.41* 58	2.95 *1.28* 768	
Developing new paved roads on forests and grasslands for access for cars and recreational vehicles.	2.32 *1.32* 96	2.39 *1.37* 1014		2.45 *1.50* 99	2.46 *1.40* 1034		3.23 *1.24* 78	3.12 *1.24* 846	
Making the permitting process easier for some established uses of forests and grasslands such as grazing, logging, mining, and commercial recreation.	2.42 *1.39* 101	2.77 *1.40* 963	**	2.58 *1.36* 95	2.66 *1.44* 1039		3.12 *1.35* 59	2.95 *1.26* 708	
Developing and maintaining continuous trail systems that cross both public and private land for motorized vehicles such as snowmobiles or ATVs.	2.56 *1.41* 116	2.80 *1.41* 1166		2.74 *1.36* 97	2.81 *1.45* 1026		3.08 *1.32* 71	3.21 *1.19* 866	
Expanding commercial recreation on forests and grasslands (for example, ski areas, guide services, or outfitters).	2.74 *1.35* 77	2.88 *1.30* 1000		2.67 *1.40* 115	3.05 *1.35* 1183	***	3.19 *1.26* 67	3.38 *1.14* 821	

[a] Standard deviation
[b] Sample size for each item (n).
*, **, *** mean differences are statistically significant at $\alpha = 0.05$, 0.01, and 0.001 respectively, based on a t-test.

Objectives Identified as Moderately Important

As was done in the earlier section exploring objectives for moderate importance for Region 5, results have been organized by issues to facilitate a discussion of related issues (for example, objectives which deal either directly or indirectly with resource extraction are grouped together). These results are reported in table 11.

Resource extraction and use—Respondents from Region 5 consistently view the objectives that deal with resource extraction and use as slightly less important than do respondents from the rest of the United States (table 11). Only one objective, dealing with the provision of natural resources to support communities dependent on grazing, mining, or timber, was ranked significantly lower (mean from Region 5, 3.21; mean from the rest of the United States, 3.58).

Respondents from Region 5 differ significantly from respondents from the rest of the United States about the appropriateness of the role for the USDA Forest Service in two of the five resource extraction and use objectives. The objective to restrict timber harvesting and grazing is evaluated as a more appropriate role for the USDA Forest Service by the respondents from Region 5, while on the other hand, preserving the cultural uses of forests and grasslands is evaluated as less appropriate.

Finally, the public in Region 5 and the respondents from the rest of the United States generally agree on how favorably they view the performance of the USDA Forest Service in fulfilling resource extraction and use objectives. The only evaluation with a statistically significant difference, involving restricting mineral development on forests and grasslands, showed respondents from Region 5 viewing the USDA Forest Service's performance on restricting mineral development less favorably.

Table 11--Comparison of the objectives, beliefs, and attitudes identified as moderately important by Region 5 with the rest of the United States.

OBJECTIVE	Is this an important objective for you? (1=not at all important, 5=very important)			Do you believe that fulfilling this objective is an appropriate role for the USDA Forest Service? (1=strongly disagree, 5=strongly agree)			How favorably do you view the performance of the USDA Forest Service in fulfilling this objective? (1=very unfavorably, 5=very favorably)		
	Region 5	Rest of US	Sig. diff –R5/rest US	Region 5	Rest of US	Sig. diff –R5/rest US	Region 5	Rest of US	Sig. diff –R5/rest US
Resource Extraction and Use Objectives									
Restricting mineral development on forests and grasslands.	3.99 *1.20*[a] 88[b]	4.00 *1.29* 1004		3.81 *1.48* 102	3.95 *1.33* 1021		2.87 *1.34* 67	3.33 *1.35* 861	****
Restricting timber harvesting and grazing on forests and grasslands.	3.83 *1.33* 94	3.97 *1.25* 1048		4.26 *1.08* 91	3.91 *1.32* 980	***	3.20 *1.20* 79	3.31 *1.30* 867	
Preserving the cultural uses of forests and grasslands by Native Americans and Native Hispanics such as firewood gathering, her/berry/plant gathering, and ceremonial access.	3.66 *1.39* 129	3.79 *1.28* 1225		3.41 *1.40* 107	3.67 *1.30* 1356	**	3.53 *1.07* 83	3.38 *1.23* 937	
Designating more wilderness areas on public land that stops access for development and motorized uses.	3.58 *1.47* 77	3.87 *1.28* 998		3.69 *1.43* 102	3.66 *1.41* 1989		3.51 *1.11* 75	3.27 *1.25* 826	
Providing natural resources from forests and grasslands to support communities dependent on grazing, mining, or timber harvesting.	3.21 *1.35* 89	3.58 *1.32* 1017	**	3.02 *1.44* 82	3.27 *1.35* 994		3.31 *1.19* 89	3.35 *1.16* 955	
Public Relations and Management Objectives									
Informing the public on the economic value received by developing our natural resources.	3.94 *1.34* 99	4.03 *1.22* 1013		3.54 *1.38* 96	4.03 *1.18* 975	****	3.08 *1.29* 77	3.22 *1.30* 909	
Making management decisions concerning the use of forests and grasslands at the local level rather than at the national level.	3.78 *1.16* 73	4.00 *1.16* 844		3.74 *1.31* 90	3.95 *1.20* 1053		3.18 *1.23* 68	3.43 *1.26* 737	
Recreation Objectives									
Developing and maintaining continuous trail systems that cross both public and private land for non-motorized recreation such as hiking or cross-country skiing.	3.82 *1.24*[a] 100[b]	3.71 *1.27* 1033		3.72 *1.25* 83	3.67 *1.31* 1042		3.48 *1.07* 61	3.60 *1.16* 859	
Increasing law enforcement efforts by public land agencies on public land.	3.73 *1.29* 79	3.90 *1.21* 883		3.90 *1.24* 92	4.03 *1.16* 882		3.69 *1.14* 68	3.64 *1.23* 724	
Designating some existing recreation trails for specific use (for example, creating separate trails for snowmobiling and cross-country skiing or for mountain biking and horseback riding).	3.51 *1.30* 88	3.69 *1.32* 1032		3.78 *1.17* 88	3.93 *1.18* 983		3.48 *1.14* 85	3.58 *1.18* 879	
Paying an entry fee that goes to support public land.	3.38 *1.43* 79	3.62 *1.29* 856		3.71 *1.27* 89	3.64 *1.29* 887		3.57 *1.30* 76	3.50 *1.23* 739	

Table 11. *Continued.*

Land Acquisition Objectives						
Increasing the total number of acres in the public land system.	3.69 *1.42* 68	3.67 *1.34* 897	4.09 *1.27* 70	3.80 *1.33* 883	3.29 *1.37* 68	3.42 *1.20* 741
Allowing public land managers to trade public lands for private lands (for example, to eliminate private property within public land boundaries, or to acquire unique areas of land.)	3.26 *1.40* 68	3.09 *1.38* 770	3.43 *1.36* 74	3.20 *1.39* 792	3.02 *1.18* 55	3.16 *1.22* 740

[a] Standard deviation
[b] Sample size for each item (n).
*, **, ***, **** mean differences are statistically significant at $\alpha = 0.10, 0.05, 0.01$, and 0.001 respectively, based on a t-test.

Public relations and management—The respondents from Region 5 agree with the respondents from the rest of the United States concerning the level of importance for the two objectives of moderate importance that deal with public relations and management (table 11). However, the respondents from Region 5 view informing the public about economic values as a significantly less appropriate objective for the Forest Service than do respondents from the rest of the United States (mean for Region 5, 3.54, mean for the rest of the United States, 4.03). Region 5 respondents' lower mean is paired with a higher standard deviation, showing less agreement among the respondents of Region 5 than those from the rest of the United States (s.d. for Region 5, 1.38, s.d. for the rest of the United States, 1.18).

Despite statistically significant differences with views of appropriateness of the role for the USDS Forest Service, people from Region 5 are in agreement with people from the rest of the United States when it comes to evaluating agency performance for public relations and management.

Recreation—There are no statistically significant differences between the responses from Region 5 and those of the rest of the United States for the four recreation objectives. These similar evaluations are evident not only when looking at the importance of the recreation objectives, but also when evaluating the appropriateness of the role for the USDA Forest Service, and agency performance in fulfilling the objective.

Land acquisition—There are no statistically significant differences reported between the evaluations of land acquisition objectives from Region 5 and from the rest of the United States.

Public Lands Values

Socially Responsible Individual Values

Table 12 shows the comparison between Region 5 respondent's Socially Responsible Individual Values and those of the rest of the United States. The mean scores for Region 5 do not appear to be consistently higher or lower than those for respondents from the rest of the United States. In the six cases where there are statistically significant differences, there are four cases where the respondents from Region 5 evaluated the values as higher than the rest of the United States (greater level of environmental orientation) and two cases where they evaluated them as lower.

Socially Responsible Management Values

In all cases where there is a statistically significant difference, the mean responses of Socially Responsible Management Values from Region 5 are lower than those of respondents from the rest of the United States (table 13). These statements are worded so that higher responses indicate greater value placed on the extraction and use of natural resources. Thus, respondents from Region 5 exhibit a lower preference for human-centered uses of forests and grasslands than do respondents from the rest of the United States.

Concluding Remarks_____

Data extracted from the VOBA survey reveals the Region 5 public's objectives for the management of for-

Table 12--Comparison of socially responsible individual values: Region 5 and the rest of the United States.

VALUES (1=strongly agree, 5=strongly disagree)	Region 5	Rest of US	Significant difference between Region 5 and the rest of the US
Manufacturers should be encouraged to use recycled materials in their manufacturing and processing operations.	4.76 0.69[a] 157[b]	4.64 0.80 1841	
People should be more concerned about how our public lands are used.	4.67 0.76 141	4.66 0.78 1675	
I am willing to make personal sacrifices for the sake of slowing down pollution.	4.53 0.78 155	4.35 0.95 1679	**
Future generations should be as important as the current one in the decisions about public lands.	4.54 0.91 170	4.59 0.84 1936	
Donating time or money to worthy causes is important to me.	4.38 0.91 147	4.17 1.03 1684	***
Consumers should be interested in the environmental consequences of the products they purchase.	4.48 0.93 146	4.48 0.89 1706	
I am glad there are National Forests even if I never get to see them.	4.64 0.94 181	4.75 0.71 1868	**
I am willing to stop buying products from companies that pollute the environment even though it might be inconvenient.	4.10 1.06 147	3.94 1.17 1719	
People can think public lands are valuable even if they never go there themselves.	4.42 1.07 137	4.64 0.81 1686	***
Forests have a right to exist for their own sake, regardless of human concerns and uses.	4.30 1.09 175	4.09 1.19 1777	**
People should urge their friends to limit their use of products made from scarce resources.	4.06 1.16 171	4.13 1.12 1861	
I have often thought that if we could just get by with a little less there would be more left for future generations.	4.12 1.17 137	4.03 1.22 1615	
The whole pollution issue has never upset me too much since I feel it's somewhat overrated. [c]	3.00 1.24 162	2.72 1.41 1689	**
I would be willing to sign a petition for an environmental cause.	3.97 1.30[a] 152[b]	3.87 1.36 1630	
Wildlife, plants, and humans have equal rights to live and grow.	4.06 1.34 133	4.15 1.27 1668	
Natural resources should be preserved even if people must do without some products.	4.18 1.41 150	4.09 1.17 1865	
I would be willing to pay five dollars more each time I use public lands for recreational purposes (for example, hiking, camping, hunting).	3.47 1.53 156	3.53 1.44 2055	

[a] Standard deviation
[b] Sample size for each item (n).
*, **, ***, **** mean differences are statistically significant at α =0.10, 0.05, 0.01, and 0.001 respectively, based on a t-test.

Table 13--Comparison of socially responsible management values – Region 5 and the rest of the United States.

VALUES (1=strongly agree, 5=strongly disagree)	Region 5	Rest of US	Significant difference between Region 5 and the rest of the US
The government has better places to spend money than devoting resources to a strong conservation program.	1.93 1.15[a] 194[b]	2.28 1.32 2156	****
I think that the public land managers are doing an adequate job of protecting natural resources from being overused.	3.01 1.25 158	3.09 1.18 2006	
The Federal government should subsidize the development and leasing of public lands to companies.	2.03 1.30 195	2.14 1.37 2136	
The decision to develop resources should be based mostly on economic grounds.	2.42 1.33 179	2.72 1.35 2106	***
The most important role for the public lands is providing jobs and income for local people.	2.90 1.46 210	2.92 1.39 2370	
The primary use of forests should be for products that are useful to humans.	2.64 1.46 209	2.68 1.42 2338	
The main reason for maintaining resources today is so we can use them in the future if we need to.	3.58 1.48 183	3.71 1.36 2129	
We should actively harvest more trees to meet the needs of a much larger human population.	2.49 1.51 203	2.58 1.53 2140	

[a] Standard deviation
[b] Sample size for each item (n).
*, **, ***, **** mean differences are statistically significant at α =0.10, 0.05, 0.01, and 0.001 respectively, based on a t-test.

USDA Forest Service RMRS-GTR-157. 2005.

Appendix

ests and rangelands, beliefs about whether it is the role of the Forest Service to fulfill these objectives, and attitudes about the performance of the agency in fulfilling the objectives. Additionally, these data show the public's environmental values as they relate to public lands.

The most important objective to respondents from Region 5 was a concern for conserving and protecting forest and grasslands that are the source of water resources. This is not surprising from a Region that includes California—a State that is constantly struggling with limited water supplies. Objectives not viewed as important within Region 5 mainly deal with development of access for motorized vehicles (on and off road), although the evaluations of these objectives also have a variety of diverse responses.

Finally this report also compares the responses of respondents from Region 5 to those of respondents from the rest of the United States. Overall, responses from Region 5 are quite similar to those of the rest of the United States, although Region 5 shows a stronger tendency towards allowing access for diverse uses and less of a trend toward informing the public.

Survey Design and Implementation

Between September 1999 and June 2000 over 80 focus groups and individual interviews were conducted across the lower 48 States. These efforts concentrated on three topics; 1) issues related to the use of public lands in general and forests and rangelands in particular, 2) the objectives (or goals) of the group (or individual) regarding the use, management, and conservation of the forests and rangelands, and 3) the role of the Forest Service in the use, management, and conservation of the forests and rangelands.

Based upon the results of the focus group interviews, an objectives hierarchy was constructed for each group. These hierarchies indicated what each group or individual was attempting to achieve, and how they would achieve each goal or objective. These objectives ranged from the abstract strategic level to the more specific or applied means level. The means level objectives are at the bottom of the hierarchy, while the strategic objective is at the top. Fundamental objectives between the means level and the strategic level completed the hierarchies. Therefore, the strategic level objective is an abstract objective that can be achieved by more specific fundamental level objectives, which are in turn achieved by means level objectives. (See figure 1.)

Each of the objectives hierarchies was confirmed with its respective group so as to ensure that it accurately reflected the group's goals and objectives. A combined objectives hierarchy was then constructed that included all the objectives stated by each group or individual interviewed. The result was a hierarchy that covered five strategic level objectives related to access, preservation/conservation, commodity development, education, and natural resource management. These 5 strategic level objectives were supported by 30 fundamental objectives.

The 30 fundamental level objectives were used to develop 30 objectives statements that were utilized in the National Survey of Recreation and the Environment (NSRE). The NSRE was a national survey administered via telephone interviews. The 30 objectives statements were divided into 5 groups based upon the strategic level objectives the focus groups had identified. During the telephone interviews, each respondent was asked one statement from each of the five strategic-level groups to obtain a statistically valid sample for each statement and for each strategic-level group.

The survey of the American public's values, objectives, beliefs, and attitudes (hereafter VOBA) was conducted as a module within the NSRE. Although questions about respondents' recreation behavior comprise the bulk of the interview the results presented here are based solely on the questions in the VOBA Module of the survey and the demographic questions. The VOBA questions are sets of scale items to which people are asked to respond using a 5-point scale. The objectives items are anchored by 1=not at all important to 5=very important. Beliefs are anchored by 1=strongly disagree to 5=strongly agree and attitudes are anchored by 1=very unfavorable to 5=very favorable. Each of these three scales consists of 30 items. The 25 items in the "values" scale are anchored by 1=strongly disagree and 5=strongly agree.

Reverse Scoring

When the VOBA was designed, care was taken to avoid the appearance of an instrument biased toward or against a specific position. To do this the "direction" of the scale varied. For example, for one item a "strongly agree" response might indicate a conservation/preservation orientation, while for another item the same response might indicate a development orientation. While this is useful to increase the acceptance of the instrument and subsequent response rates, it creates problems when items with the opposite direction are grouped.

To compare two or more items that have opposite directions, it is necessary to make all the items move in the same direction. For example, suppose we want to examine the overall preference for sweets as indicated by the preference for ice cream and pie. We have two scale items. For each, 1 indicates "strongly disagree" and 5 indicates "strongly agree" as in the Public Lands Values scale. To avoid the appearance of bias toward or against sweets, the two items move in opposite directions: "I like ice cream" and "I don't like pie." Clearly a person who likes all sweets will answer 5 to the first item and 1 to the second. Conversely, someone who does not like sweets will answer 1 to the first and 5 to the second. If these items are grouped, it would be more useful for research if both items are scored in the same direction to indicate preference for sweets (either with a higher or lower response for both items). To achieve this, to re-score, we choose one of the items, in this example we'll choose the second, and reverse the scoring. An answer of 5 thus becomes a 1, an answer of 4 becomes 2, 3 remains the same (neutral), 2 becomes 4, and 1 becomes 5. This in effect creates a new item (which could be reworded as "I like pie") that corresponds in direction to "I like ice cream." This re-scoring allows the researcher an overall, consistent indication of each respondent's preference for sweets. Higher numbers for each item indicate a higher preference for sweets; lower numbers indicate lower preference. A similar re-scoring was done for certain items in the VOBA to more accurately characterize overall preferences for item groups.

USDA Forest Service RMRS-GTR-157. 2005.

www.ingramcontent.com/pod-product-compliance
Lightning Source LLC
Chambersburg PA
CBHW080734290526
45790CB00008B/3196